Raspberry Pi 4 Ultimate Guide

From Beginner to Pro:

Everything You Need to Know: Setup, Programming Theory, Techniques, and Awesome Ideas to Build Your Own Projects

Ethan J. Upton

Table of Contents

Introduction

Congratulations on purchasing Raspberry Pi 4 Ultimate Guide, and thank you for doing so.

There are plenty of books on this subject on the market, thanks again for choosing this one! Every effort was made to ensure it is full of as much useful information as possible, please enjoy!

A book does not aspire to give deep theoretical knowledge but has a strictly practical orientation. We will show you what the Raspberry Pi includes, how to configure it, and how to use it to make your own projects. The examples are intended to be approachable even by first-year students who have already completed the Computer Science course.

An important incorporation in this edition of the book is the notions of software architecture. We want Raspberry Pi to be used to address real engineering problems. And for that, it is necessary that the software developed be considerably more evolved than what we usually see in the final degree projects. The examples we will address are simple but not trivial. Reusable component templates will be provided to build relatively sophisticated systems.

Info: All the code we give you with the book can be used in your own works and projects. It is distributed under the GNU public license, a permissive license that allows you to even modify the software or commercially exploit your projects. There is only one condition, and derivative works can only be distributed under this license.

An important limitation of this book is that we do not deal with strict real-time systems, but we cannot do more in two credits. In the near future, we will try to offer complementary real-time and robotics courses with Raspberry Pi.

Student Kit

This book is conceived as a pro-bono motivation activity, without any remuneration for the personnel involved in the course. 100% of the money raised in the tuition is invested in the material that the student takes. Purchases are made months in advance, thanks to the collaboration of the School of Industrial Engineering of Toledo, to take advantage of offers and foreign suppliers.

Book Structure

This book is divided into three parts:

The first part introduces the Raspberry Pi, its characteristics, its history, the operating system that we are going to use, and the development environment.

The second part describes the different components of the Raspberry Pi from an isolated point of view. It is about the student knowing how each component is programmed and what limitations it has. Finally, the last part is dedicated to software architecture issues. How we build programs that deal with multiple sources of heterogeneous events. How a complex program is organized so that it is not impossible to modify it.

Organization of this book

This little book has been divided into three parts:

- The first part is dedicated to the fundamentals and necessary introduction material. Ideally, the student should have at least this knowledge at the beginning of the book, but we will dedicate the first day to review them.

- The second part introduces peripherals and peripheral programming from an agnostic point of view regarding language. Command-line tools are used to interact with them.

- The third part is dedicated to the programming of the Raspberry Pi. Two versions are offered, one in C and one in Python. It includes material of foundations, simple examples equivalent to the second part, and case studies.

Obviously, this organization is influenced by practical aspects. We leave for the second part all the common material that we can, so as not to repeat it in the third parts C and Python. In the book, we see everything together, presenting parallel versions C and Python.

Chapter 1 - Raspberry Pi

In 2006, a group from the Computer Lab of the University of Cambridge began to worry about the level with which high school students arrived at the University. For some reason, students who had previous exposure to computer technologies accumulated knowledge about specific applications rather than knowledge about the technologies themselves. Raspberry Pi emerges as a low-cost initiative to promote experimentation with programming from an early age, although this is not a mere toy.

The Raspberry Pi Family

In the timeline above, you can see a set of the most significant milestones related to Raspberry Pi. A respectable number of models have already been generated in the short history of the Raspberry Pi Foundation:

- Raspberry Pi model B was the first model put up for sale on February 29, 2012. The original design included two models with the same printed circuit. Both were designed around a Broadcom SoC (System On a Chip), the BCM2835 at 700MHz, designed for mobile applications that require video processing or 3D graphics (video cameras, media players, mobile phones, etc.). Most of the input/output pins of the BCM2835 were arranged in a 26-pin header. Model B was the high-end, developer-oriented version with more memory (512MB of RAM versus 256MB), a 100BaseTX Ethernet port, and a USB hub with two USB 2.0 ports. The original models incorporated an SD slot. In September 2012, the design was slightly revised to correct some problems. This revision slightly modifies the available input/output pins.

- Raspberry Pi model A is the reduced version of the model B. It incorporates half of RAM than the B model (256MB), does not include an Ethernet interface and only incorporates a USB 2.0 port. It is intended for final applications where consumption and/or cost are important factors.

- The Raspberry Pi logo is a registered trademark of the Raspberry Pi Foundation. It was designed by Paul Bleech, who won the logo competition organized by the foundation in 2011. Most of the candidates are still available in the forum of the foundation. Beware of the logo; it has very strict rules of use. You cannot use it where you see fit.

- In April 2014, the Raspberry Pi Compute Module is announced. It is similar to the B model, but instead of the SD slot, it incorporates 4GB of eMMC Flash and integrates everything into a DDR2 SODIMM printed circuit, similar to that of notebook memories. This allows all the pins of the BCM2835 to be available but requires another printed circuit with the SODIMM socket and the necessary connectors. It is used extensively in the development of products based on Raspberry Pi, such as the FiveNinjas Slice media player, the CubeSat satellites, the Otto camera, the Cube Solver that is capable of solving a Rubik, Sphinx cube that is used to use a tablet as a desktop computer, etc.

- In July 2014, the Raspberry Pi model B + is announced. It is a redesign of model B, very similar but with important consequences. The number of GPIO header pins is expanded to 40 pins, the SD socket is replaced by a microSD, the number of USB ports is increased to four, the power and audio are improved, the output is included in the same connector of composite video and audio (like many laptops), and the form factor is corrected so that it fits completely into the size of a credit card. The extension of the pin header is complemented shortly afterwards with the specification HAT (Hardware Attached on Top). Compute Module IO Board with the module inserted, which determines the physical and electrical limitations that Raspberry Pi expansion boards must meet to ensure future compatibility. All Raspberry Pi will be compatible with this specification from this date. HAT allows automatic configuration of digital inputs/outputs as well as drivers through two dedicated pins (ID_SD and ID_SC). Today, there are many HATs on the market (as an example, see the collection of Adafruit, Pimoroni, and The Pi Hut). In addition to the BCM2835, the B + model incorporates an SMS95 LAN9514 that incorporates the Ethernet interface and the USB hub occupying a single USB port of the BCM2835.

- In November 2014, the Raspberry Pi A + as the equivalent redesign of model A, without SMSC LAN9514. A significant change is that the idea of using the same printed circuit is abandoned. In this way, it is possible to reduce the size significantly and with it the price. It incorporates the HAT header, which will already be present in all subsequent models, and consumption is significantly reduced.

- Almost on the third anniversary of the original Raspberry Pi, the Raspberry Pi 4 is announced. Upgrade the processor to a BCM2836 (quad-core Cortex-A7) at 900MHz and incorporate 1GB of RAM. For the first time, the possibility of using Microsoft Windows 10 on Raspberry Pi opens, although the operating system recommended by the Raspberry Pi Foundation remains Raspbian.

- This is a tiny version of the A + model with greater speed (1GHz) and more memory (512MB). Without populating the baseboards, the price was lowered to $ 5. The 40th issue of The MagPi magazine included a Raspberry Pi 4 gift. It seems that Google's pressure after a meeting of Eric Schmidt and Eben Upton was decisive in its development. However, it is a model produced directly by Raspberry Pi Trading, which has relatively limited production capacity, making it difficult to achieve.

- In 2019, the Raspberry Pi 4 B is announced, coinciding with the fourth birthday of the Raspberry Pi original model B. The change is very important because it is passed to a 64-bit architecture, although backward compatibility remains total. In addition to the BCM2837, it incorporates a BCM43438 that implements all the new wireless communication capabilities. Just leave the FM radio receiver unconnected.

- In February 2016, Eben Upton announced in various forums that a Compute Module 3 is being prepared, and it will be a Raspberry Pi 4. The specifications are not public yet, but beta versions are already available for some engineers.

If you want to know more about the history of Raspberry Pi and its community, we recommend you visit the website of The MagPi magazine. It is a magazine of great quality and completely free in its electronic version. It is also a very interesting source of suppliers of products related to Raspberry Pi.

Broadcom Chip Systems

This on-chip system incorporates a low-power ARM1176JZF-S core and a VideoCore IV dual-core multimedia coprocessor (GPU). The GPU implements OpenGL-ES 2.0 and is capable of encoding and decoding FullHD video at 30fps while displaying FullHD graphics at 60fps on an LCD or on an HDMI monitor.

A striking feature of this processor is its assembly stacked with RAM (package on package). The structure is shown in the figure. For this reason, the Raspberry Pi printed circuit does not show any processor. This technique allows for reducing the size of the PCB considerably.

This on-chip system incorporates a low-power ARM1176JZF-S core and a VideoCore IV dual-core multimedia coprocessor (GPU). The GPU implements OpenGL-ES 2.0 and is capable of encoding and decoding FullHD video at 30fps while displaying FullHD graphics at 60fps on an LCD or on an HDMI monitor. A striking feature of this processor is its assembly stacked with RAM (package on package). For this reason, the Raspberry Pi printed circuit does not show any processor.

This technique allows for reducing considerably the size of the PCB (Printed Circuit Board) necessary. In addition to the processor and the GPU, the Raspberry Pi SoC incorporates a wide array of peripherals:

- Timer
- Interrupt controller
- Generic purpose digital inputs/outputs, GPIO (General Purpose Input-Output). It has 54, but not all are available on the Raspberry Pi.
- USB port.
- PCM audio via the I2S bus (Integrated Interchip Sound).
- Direct memory access controller, DMA.
- Master and slave of I2C bus (Inter-Integrated Circuit).
- SPI bus master and slave (Serial Peripheral Interface).
- Module for generating variable width pulses, PWM.
- Serial ports, UART.
- Interface for eMMC, SD, SDIO memories.
- HDMI interface

Applying reverse engineering techniques, a substantial part of the GPU was documented in the Herman Hermitage GitHub repository. This work may have influenced Broadcom's recent decision to release the official VideoCore IV documentation. Advanced users can now enjoy reasonably mature development libraries and an accelerated OpenGL driver completely free.

The BCM2836 of the Raspberry Pi 4 has basically the same internal architecture as its predecessor but incorporates a quad-core Cortex-A7 processor that replaces the ARM117JZF-S of the BCM2835 and does not use the package-on-package assembly technique. It has important consequences from the point of view of the software since this processor implements the instruction repertoire of ARM v.7 instead of ARM v.6 as its predecessor.

The BCM2837 of the Raspberry Pi 4 B is an on-chip system designed specifically for this Raspberry Pi model. It updates the processor for four 64-bit Cortex-A53 cores but continues to incorporate the VideoCore IV GPU because it is one of the few GPUs with public documentation from the manufacturer.

The ARM Cortex-A53 has an internal name Apollo and is often used in high-performance processors in combination with the ARM Cortex-A57 (Atlas) following the big.LITTLE (heterogeneous multiprocessor) configuration. The A53 is the version of low consumption, reduced size, and relative simplicity of the ARMv8 architecture, while A57 is the version of high performance, high consumption, and larger size of the same architecture. For example, the Exynos 7 Octa or Snapdragon 810 that incorporate many high-end mobile phones follow this configuration using four cores of each type. In the case of BCM2837, it is decided to include only four low-consumption cores, so it does not intend to compete in high performance, but in energy efficiency. Basically, the expected performance is somewhat better than a quad-core Cortex-A9 (for example, like the Apple iPad 2 processor) but at a significantly lower cost.

A Raspberry Pi for the Book

This initiation book could be carried out on any Raspberry Pi model. The new Raspberry Pi 4 is ideal for equipment prototypes, but it makes development difficult. For example, connecting a keyboard and mouse would require a USB OTG hub. The mere update of the operating system would require some kind of network connection, and connecting external devices to the GPIO port requires incorporating pin headers or soldering. All this is already in the Raspberry Pi model B +.

The added cost of all the additional components that would be necessary to incorporate the Raspberry Pi 4 to develop comfortably far exceeds the cost of the Raspberry Pi B +.

Unfortunately, the price of the B + model is rising due to the fall in demand since the Raspberry Pi 4 is launched. At this juncture, the Raspberry Pi 4 B is released at the same price as the Raspberry Pi 4, but also including WiFi and Bluetooth interface. For this reason, we decided to include the new Raspberry 3 model B in this edition. However, all book examples are compatible with any of the models.

Interoperability with Other Products

Around the Raspberry Pi Foundation has emerged a huge community of users of all levels that generates information and products. Today there are specific peripherals of all kinds for Raspberry Pi. There are cameras, touch panels with TFT screen, and many interface cards with other devices.

It is worth noting the efforts to integrate peripherals from other platforms that already enjoyed a wide user community. For example, Lego Mindstorms peripherals and LEGO Technic parts can be used to build Raspberry Pi controlled robots using BrickPi from Dexter Industries.

The huge variety of Arduino expansion modules (shields) can also be used with GertDuino from Gert van Loo, or with Arduberry from Dexter Industries, or with AlaMode from WyoLum or with ArduPi from Cooking Hacks. The tandem of Raspberry Pi and Arduino is very interesting when strict latency control is required. The Raspbian GNU / Linux operating system is not real-time, it cannot guarantee very low interrupt latencies, and the resolution of the timers is of the order of milliseconds. However, the greater simplicity of Arduino software makes it very predictable in terms of response times.

Finally, we would like to mention the Raspberry Pi to Grove interfaces, modular and open architecture for building LEGO-style electronic systems in physical systems. Grove was initially designed to be compatible with Arduino, and therefore can be used together with the adapters mentioned above, but can also be used directly using GrovePi from Dexter Industries, a shield base specially designed for Raspberry Pi.

Chapter 2 - The GNU / Linux System

The Raspberry Pi has a complete operating system, with graphics environment and programming tools of various types. We will use this environment to carry out most of the book. However, we must specify that the usual way of developing embedded systems is to use a PC and program the Raspberry Pi remotely.

GNU / Linux is the usual name of the operating system that the Raspberry Pi carries. Raspbian and Debian are nothing more than distributions of this operating system. That is, Raspbian is a selection of GNU / Linux packages, compiled for a specific architecture, and packaged with the help of specific tools to achieve a pleasant user experience. Instead of going here and there in search of installers and drivers as we do in Microsoft Windows, GNU specializes in packages for specific purposes.

GNU is the correct name of the operating system. It means GNU's Not Unix, that is, GNU is not Unix. It is a recursive acronym. It refers to the fact that it does not contain a single line of Unix, the proprietary operating system of AT&T, which then sold to SCO and licensed to multiple international brands. The Linux suffix refers to the kernel of the operating system. GNU has its own kernel, the HURD, but is not yet ready for general use. That's why most distributions add to GNU some of the free kernels out there (Linux, FreeBSD, NetBSD, etc.)

Info: In 1983, Richard M. Stallman, who worked as a researcher at the AI Lab at MIT, decided to start the GNU project in order to make unnecessary the use of any other non-free software. It is still far from reaching its goal, but GNU is already used in many electronic devices. You can read more about the initial objective of the project, The GNU Manifesto.

In 1985 he created the Free Software Foundation with the aim of spreading the free software movement and helping the development of the GNU system. Listen to Richard Stallman himself explaining the philosophy of the movement.

As soon as you connect the Raspberry Pi to the power, it will start in a graphic environment like the one at the beginning of the chapter. The following elements appear at the top.

- Applications menu
- Order line terminal.
- Raspberry Pi configuration tool.
- File management tool.
- Integrated Python development environment (IDLE).
- Text editor
- Basic web browser.

From the menu, it is possible to run most of the installed applications. However, with the quick launch buttons of applications, we will have enough for most of the book activities.

The File System

Let's first get acquainted with the structure of folders and files of the system. To do this, click on the quick launch button of the file manager.

The text box at the top indicates /home /pi, which is the current folder. The routes of the files and folders use the character / as a separator. It's not possible to have a folder with that character in the name because the system could not differentiate it from a route of two components. The folder / without more is the root folder, where everything hangs. Not here. Here, there are unit names, all units are seen at some point in the tree of folders that are born in the root folder. The route /home/pi refers to being found in the pi folder of the File Manager. As you can imagine, it is the personal folder. The name 'home' refers to the folder containing all the personal folders (home in English). And inside that folder, the folder pi is that of the user pi. Indeed, pi is the name of the user created folder by default in the system when installed. In the book, we will use this user exclusively, but we encourage you to become your own user. You will see that in this folder, there are already some files. They are examples of programs in several programming languages, which we will use in the course.

Although the system does not require it, the different variants of GNU tend to maintain a common folder structure.

For example, the following are usually present in almost all GNU systems:

/ home / Personal folders of users.
/ root / Personal folder of the administrator (root user).
/ etc / System configuration files.
/ boot / Files needed for system boot.
/ bin / Basic orders (system executables).
/ usr / bin / Rest of system orders (executables).
/ lib / Basic system libraries
/ usr / lib / Other system libraries.
/ usr / local / Software installed manually, not belonging to the system.
/ tmp / Temporary folder.
/ dev / System devices. In GNU all devices are viewed as special files.

Use the file manager to navigate the system and familiarize yourself with it. Do not worry, as a pi user, you cannot destroy anything essential to the system. We propose the following exercises:

1. Find the file wpa_supplicant.conf. This is the file where you can configure the WiFi network so that the Raspberry Pi automatically connects to your access

point.

2. Find the flickering.py file that is an example program written in Python that we will use in the course.
3. Find the gcc program. This is the C compiler.
4. Find the idle program. This is the integrated programming environment with Python.

Warning

Traditionally in operating systems, the term directory is used to refer to a folder. In the same way, many texts in Spanish speak of files to refer to files. We will try to use the term folder that best fits the metaphor of the desktop.

A file is one of those cardboard folders that get into office filing cabinets. The problem is that the files cannot also be called a folder. That is why more neutral translations were sought. The file is really the archive, rather than the contents of the archive. But we warn you because in the documentation you read there, it is easy for them to appear. The directory is the same as a folder, and the file is the same as file.

The Command-Line Environment

Execute the command line terminal by clicking on the corresponding icon. Although apparently, it is a primitive interface, this is one of the most flexible ways to communicate with the operating system.

Pressing the icon, we will see that a new window opens. That window corresponds to the terminal simulator program. It behaves like an old console with a keyboard and alphanumeric screen. In turn, the terminal program runs another program that is responsible for interpreting textual commands, the shell.

In GNU / Linux, the shell that is normally used is called bash (Bourne Again Shell). It has many features that make it a complete programming language by itself. We will not see the advanced features, but some basic notions that will allow you to unfold with ease during the course.

When the shell is executed, a small text appears before the cursor; it is the prompt.

Raspberry Pi pi @: ~ $ ▄

Before the colon appears, the user and the name of the computer simulating an email address. Before the @ symbol, the name of the user who runs the shell appears. In this case, the user is pi, which is the default user, and the one we will use in our examples. Then the hostname appears, which we have configured in the installation as rpi.

After the colon and before the $ symbol,   the work folder appears. The working folder (or directory) is that folder in which the shell is currently located. All processes have a working folder, and the shell is no exception. It is used as a basis to determine the files that are located by relative paths. We will see this right away.

The ~ symbol is an abbreviation for the user's home folder. In this case / home / pi. This abbreviation can be used in any order that needs a route.

There are many highly recommended references to understand the shell and exploit its full potential. An excellent book available for free is available at tldp.org.

File Management

All operations that can be performed with the file manager can also be performed with commands in the shell. Let's see a brief summary of the most frequent orders.

File list: ls

The most basic file management operation is to display the contents of a folder. It is done with the ls (list) command.

Without further arguments, it shows the contents of the working folder (the one that appears in the prompt).

The colors of each element tell us what it is. Folders are shown in blue, normal files in gray, and executables in green. By default, it does not show hidden elements, which are those whose name begins with. (point). You can indicate as an argument the folder or folders whose content you want to list:

pi @ raspberrypi: ~ $ ls src
c python README.md
Raspberry Pi pi @: ~ $ ▃

It is assumed that you want to list the src folder within the current folder. It is what is known as a relative path and is assumed to be relative to the working folder. You can also indicate the full path /home/pi/src, which is known as the absolute path. As we said before, the symbol ~ is an abbreviation of the user's home folder. Therefore, another way to express the full path would be ~ / src.

And to see hidden files and folders you can use the -a option:

pi @ raspberrypi: ~ $ ls src -a
... c.git python README.md
Raspberry Pi pi @: ~ $ ▃

In this case, the .git folder is hidden. Dot folders have a special meaning for the operating system and appear in all system folders. Folder. it represents the same folder in which it is located, and the folder.. represents the folder that contains the one shown. In our example, the src /.. folder is /home/pi while the.. folder would be / home. The src/folder. It is the same as./src, the same as src and the same as /home/pi/ src in our example.

Like all other orders, ls allows you to specify various options that modify their behavior. These options are preceded by a hyphen and can be combined or indicated separately.

If this option has not resolved your doubts, use man (book). It is a tool available in all Unix variants to consult the electronic version of the reference book. And if you have doubts about how to use man? Don't think about it, use man - help, and if it's not enough, remember that to exit man, you have to press the q (quit) key.

We have installed the book pages in Spanish. If there is help in Spanish, you will see it in Spanish. If not, practice English, if you use Raspberry Pi, it will be very useful to know English.

In some cases, there are several book pages for the same concept. For example, printf is a shell order, but it is also a C function, and you probably have the version in Spanish and English. The book pages are grouped into sections, the original sections of the Unix reference book. You can tell man what section you want to refer (a number from 1 to 9) to. For example:

pi @ raspberrypi: ~ $ man 3 printf
You have the complete list of sections on the man book page, and you don't need to know it by heart.

Some man options worth highlighting:

Option	Meaning
-k	Search for the keyword indicated in the book pages and show the ones that contain it
-K	Show all applicable book pages
-to	Pipes and redirects

The standard output of a program may be too large. So big that even with the terminal scroll bar, you could see everything. In those cases, you may be interested in redirecting the output to a file for reading carefully with an editor. For example, we will generate a file with all the executables of the system:

pi @ raspberrypi: ~ $ ls -1 / bin> exe-bin.txt
pi @ raspberrypi: ~ $ ls -1 / usr / bin> exe-usr-bin.txt
pi @ raspberrypi: ~ $ ls -1 / usr / local / bin> exe-usr-local-bin.txt
Raspberry Pi pi @: ~ $ ▃

When using the symbol >, we are telling the shell that when I have to write something by standard output, write it in the indicated file. In our example, when the ls program executes a call to printf or similar, what it writes goes directly at the end of the indicated file. Now we can see these files carefully using an editor, such as Leafpad:

pi @ raspberrypi: ~ $ leafpad exe-bin.txt

And if we want to count how many executables the system has in total? We could use the wc program that counts, among other things, the lines of a file.

For example:
pi @ raspberrypi: ~ $ wc -l exe - *. txt
158 exe-bin.txt
1168 exe-usr-bin.txt
1 exe-usr-local-bin.txt
1327 total

Raspberry Pi pi @: ~ $ ▄

We can also redirect the standard input of a program. For example:
pi @ raspberrypi: ~ $ wc -l <exe-bin.txt
158
pi @ raspberrypi: ~ $ wc -l <exe-usr-bin.txt
1168
pi @ raspberrypi: ~ $ wc -l <exe-usr-local-bin.txt
Raspberry Pi pi @: ~ $ ▄

Now wc does not indicate any file name because it does not know it; the content of the file arrives directly when calling scanf or something similar. The good thing is that the result is a simple number that may be more convenient for other things.

But if we are interested in knowing how many executables there are and we are not interested in what specific files they are, why do we keep the list of executables in files? GNU is possible to connect the standard output of a program to the standard input of another program establishing what is known as a pipe (pipe in English):
pi @ raspberrypi: ~ $ ls -1 / bin / usr / bin / usr / local / bin | wc -l 1327
Raspberry Pi pi @: ~ $ ▄

The symbol | connects the standard output of the order on the left with the standard input of the order on the right. Even if we want to examine the list of executables, we can use this construction to avoid having to save the intermediate file:

pi @ raspberrypi: ~ $ ls -1 / bin / usr / bin / usr / local / bin | less

The less program is a pager, a program that shows what comes through standard page-by-page input. With the arrow keys or with space, we can go through all the information, and when we have finished examining it, just exit by pressing the q key.

But the programs not only have a standard output. They also have a standard error output. When they show an error, they usually show it by this error output. Normally it is the same terminal, and we see the error messages mixed with the program output. But we can separate it:

pi @ raspberrypi: ~ $ ls -R / etc 2> errors.txt /etc/:
adduser.conf
...
Raspberry Pi pi @: ~ $ ▄

The number 2 refers to the file descriptor corresponding to the standard error output, while the number 1 (or nothing) refers to the file descriptor of the standard output. We will talk about file descriptors when we get to the programming part of the book.

If we are only interested in errors, we can discard the standard output by redirecting it to the special file / dev / null:

pi @ raspberrypi: ~ $ ls -R / etc> / dev / null
ls: cannot open the directory / etc / polkit-1 / localauthority: Permission denied
ls: cannot open the / etc / ssl / private: Permission denied
Raspberry Pi pi @: ~ $ ▄

As a pi user, we cannot do anything. The problem with this order is that if there are many mistakes, we lose the first, which are usually the most important. Can we use a pager? No, because the pipes only connect standard output with standard input. The solution is to connect the standard error output with the same standard output, wherever you go.

pi @ raspberrypi: ~ $ ls -R / etc 2> & 1 1> / dev / null | less

Redirect descriptor 2 (standard error) to descriptor 1 (standard output), descriptor 1 (standard output) to / dev / null (discard) and connect the new standard output (new descriptor 1 which is the old error output) to the standard paginator input less.

Or without discarding the standard output, combining it together with the standard error output:

pi @ raspberrypi: ~ $ ls -R / etc 2> & 1 | less

This last form of redirection is extraordinarily useful when programming in C language. When compiling programs appear, messages from the compilation tool and also compiler errors. It is usually a lot of text, we need to see it with a pager, and we are especially interested in the first mistakes.

In addition to the pagers, it is advisable to comment in this section some filters. A filter is nothing more than a program that receives the standard input of another program, manipulates it in a certain way, and returns it to sacrifice once manipulated by the standard output.

An extraordinarily useful filter is grep (global regular expression print). It is an order that looks for lines that contain a certain pattern. Lines that do not contain the pattern are not printed, while those that contain it are printed. For example, to find all executables of / usr / bin that contain zip in the name:

pi @ raspberrypi: ~ $ ls -R / usr / bin | grep zip
Raspberry Pi pi @: ~ $ ▄

You can change the operation to print the lines that do not meet the pattern or write much more evolved patterns. When you can take some time to understand the operation of grep by reading the page of the book.

Links: In

A file has two clearly distinct parts: a name and a content. The name allows you to easily organize and find the files, but once you have found a program, you can open it (for example, with the fopen function if we are programming in C) and forget the name completely.

The idea that the name is a mere organizational device leads us to wonder if we could use several names for the same file. The answer is yes, with a link. The simplest form of link makes the source file of the destination file indistinguishable. Examine in detail this sequence of orders:

pi @ raspberrypi: ~ $ echo "First test"> a.txt
pi @ raspberrypi: ~ $ cat a.txt
First test
pi @ raspberrypi: ~ $ ln a.txt b.txt
pi @ raspberrypi: ~ $ echo "Second test"> b.txt
pi @ raspberrypi: ~ $ cat a.txt
Second test
Raspberry Pi pi @: ~ $ ▪

The ln a.txt b.txt command has created a new b.txt name for the same a.txt file. That is why when we write in b.txt, the result can also be seen in a.txt.

The problem is that this form of link does not work with folders, which are also organizational entities without other content than the names of their files. It also wouldn't work with files that are in another file system, such as a USB skewer.
To solve these problems are the symbolic links (option -s):

pi @ raspberrypi: ~ $ ln -s src / c / reactor reactor
pi @ raspberrypi: ~ $ ls -l reactor
reactor -> src / c / reactor
Raspberry Pi pi @: ~ $ ▪

A symbolic link is simply an indication that that name really corresponds to the content labeled with another name. This solves the above problems, but the file and the link are no longer equivalent. If the file is deleted, the link hangs (dangling link), and any attempt to access will cause an error.

Symbolic links are very useful to simplify folder browsing. The last example we showed lines above is illustrative of this. If we are working with a folder continuously (reactor), it is logical to leave it more by hand in our home.

Users and Permissions

You have already noticed that as a pi user, you do not have permission to do anything. We will look in more detail at the Unix permission model and how you can skip restrictions when necessary.

The uid is the user identifier, while the gid is the group identifier. All users have a uid and a gid. However, a user can belong to many groups, as shown at the end of the id output. There is a special user, the super-user, who has the uid 0 and has no permissions limitation.

We will now examine in more detail this order ls that we saw earlier:

pi @ raspberrypi: ~ $ ls src / README.md -l
-rw-r - r-- 1 pi pi 55 Apr 11 08:26 src / README.md
Raspberry Pi pi @: ~ $ ▬

Until now, we had only seen the date and time of the last modification. However, before the date, there is much more information.

Countryside   Meaning

-rw-r - r--	Permissions
One	Number of references to the file (names or links)
Pi	User (owner)
Pi	Group (owner)
55	Size in bytes
Apr 11 08:26	Date and Time

Permissions are represented in an abbreviated notation that corresponds directly to the internal representation in the file system.

The first character represents the type of file. It is d   for directories, - for normal files, l for symbolic links, or other letters that represent other types of files (devices of various types, pipes, sockets, etc.).

The following characters are divided into three-letter groups that represent the permissions for the user who owns the file, for the group that owns the file and for everyone else, in this order. Each block of three letters represents four possible permissions, according to the following table. A script in any of the letters represents the absence of the corresponding permission.

Structure of the permissions of a file in GNU.

Excuse me		Representation
Reading	r	in the first letter
Writing	w	in the second letter
Execution	x	in the third letter
Set-id	s	in the third letter (only in user group or group)
Sticky	t	in the third letter (only in a group of others)

The read permission allows you to see the contents of the file to the corresponding group. In our example, the three groups (owner-user, owner group, and others) can read the file. That is, we can execute the cat order, or read it with an editor as Leafpad. In the case of folders, the read permission allows you to see the content, that is, do ls. Write permission allows changes to the file. In our example, only the owner pi can modify it, because none of the other permission groups have the letter w. In a folder, it means that we can add or delete items (other files or folders).

Execution permission allows you to execute the file. It is this and nothing else that makes a file executable. In GNU, there are no special extensions to identify executables. In the folders, it means that we can access what is contained in them. That implies both making a CD and accessing in any way the content of what is in the folder (see the size or owner of a file, display the content, or list a subfolder).

The set-id permission is used to set the uid or gid to the owner of the file when it is executed. That is, if an executable has the set-id permission for the owner user, then when it is executed, it does so with the permissions of that owner user (temporarily changes its uid) and not with the permissions of the user who executes it. It is a way of assigning permissions for certain operations to other users, to all who have permission to execute the file. The same can be done with the set-id permission for the owner group. When the file is executed, it does so as if the user who executed it belonged to the group that owns the file (temporarily changes its gid. This permission is normally called setuid or setgid, depending on whether it applies to the owner user or the owner group.

The sticky permission (sticky in English) has changed its meaning with the historical evolution of Unix. Nowadays, it is very useful for folders. A folder with sticky permission does not allow the files contained to be deleted or renamed by users other than the owner. It is used, for example, in the temporary folder / tmp so that some users cannot cause problems to others.

We have changed the group of the file to users, which is one of the groups to which we belong, and then we have added the write permission to the owner group. Now all users belonging to the users group can edit the archive. The order allows you to add permissions or remove them for the owner user. You can also combine both the group to which the permission applies and the permissions that apply. With -R it is applied recursively. For example:

pi @ raspberrypi: ~ $ chmod -R ug + rwX src
Raspberry Pi pi @: ~ $ ▂

Notice that the execution permit has been capitalized instead of lower case. That has a special meaning. When chmod is told X instead of x, we are telling him to only apply that permission to folders, not files.

The Super User

The super-user is the user with zero uid, which usually has the name of root. This user does not apply permission restrictions. You can do everything; you are the system administrator. Obviously, it is necessary to be an administrator to be able to do certain things, such as updating the system, installing new software, etc. But it will also be necessary to use some peripherals of the Raspberry Pi. For example, to read or change the values of the GPIO legs (General Purpose Input Output).

In Raspberry Pi, it is considered so necessary that it is configured to be extremely simple to become superuser. Just run sudo su:
pi @ raspberrypi: ~ $ sudo su
pi @ raspberrypi: ~ # id
uid = 0 (root) gid = 0 (root) groups = 0 (root)
Raspberry Pi pi @: ~ # ▂

See how the prompt has changed. A # appears that should be interpreted as a severe warning. Watch out!

You can destroy everything!
Try to minimize the time you are as a superuser. It is not uncommon to completely destroy the system software by mistake, and you would have to install everything from scratch.

The sudo (superuser do) order allows certain users and with certain restrictions to execute any system order as a superuser. As you can imagine is a program that has permission setuid to root. Needless run sudo su, you can run sudo, followed by anything we have to do as a superuser. For example:

pi @ raspberrypi: ~ $ sudo chown root executable
pi @ raspberrypi: ~ $ sudo chmod u + s executable
Raspberry Pi pi @: ~ $ ▬

We have changed the owner of an executable using the chown order. As superuser, we can change anything. We have put root as the new owner (the superuser) and have added the setuid permission. This one executable moment is executed with superuser permissions.

Process Management

One of the activities that you should surely do when you are developing is to see what processes are running in the system and stop processes that may have been blocked. We will comment on only three applications for these purposes, although the range of tools is much wider. Do not stay in what we tell you, learn little by little more tools.

First of all, to see the processes that are running in the system is the order ps (processes). Without any additional argument, it provides us with information on the processes that have been executed from the same shell in which it is executed.

ps:
pi @ raspberrypi: ~ $ ps
PID   TTY   TIME CMD
894   pts / 0 00:00:18   bash
1211   pts / 0 00:00:00   ps
Raspberry Pi pi @: ~ $ ▬

In a tabular format, basic information is shown:

Countryside	Meaning
PID	Process identifier
TTY	Terminal
TIME	CPU accumulated time
CMD	Executable name

The pid (process id) is a number that assigns the operating system to all processes. Each running process must have a different pid, but once finished, its old pid can be used in another process. We can control the processes using this identification number. Let's illustrate with an example. Open a terminal and type:

pi @ raspberrypi: ~ $ cat
The cat process is waiting for data from its standard input, but we will assume that we have no idea what happens. We only know that the program does not end. We are going to kill him.

Run another terminal and type:
pi @ raspberrypi: ~ $ ps -u pi | grep cat
2093 pts / 0 00:00:00 cat
Raspberry Pi pi @: ~ $ ▬

We show all user processes pi (option -u) but then filter the output with grep to show only the lines that contain cat. The first number is the PID of the process. We will request its termination with the kill order:

pi @ raspberrypi: ~ $ kill 2093
Raspberry Pi pi @: ~ $ ▃

If you look at the first terminal, the process is over and indicates it on the screen with a message.

pi @ raspberrypi: ~ $ cat
Finished
Raspberry Pi pi @: ~ $ ▃

The program may not end. We can still do something else, and we can demand that the program end. If he doesn't do it this time, the operating system will kill him. Run cat again and in the other window:

pi @ raspberrypi: ~ $ ps -u pi | grep cat
2101 pts / 0 00:00:00 cat
pi @ raspberrypi: ~ $ kill -9 2101
Raspberry Pi pi @: ~ $ ▃

Now the message that shows the other window is slightly different:
pi @ raspberrypi: ~ $ cat
Finished
Raspberry Pi pi @: ~ $ ▃

The kill command is not exactly to kill processes. Actually, kill sends signals to the processes. There are a lot of signals that can be sent (use the -l option to have a list). By default, it sends signal 15 (SIGTERM) that it is a termination request. The processes can ignore it. Option -9 simply sends a different signal (SIGKILL) that processes cannot ignore.

It is also advisable to comment on the top order, which shows the state of the system in real time, putting the processes that more memory and / or CPU consume in the first place. If the system is slow and you don't know why you might have left some hanging process. Look to top what is and kill him. Once identified, you can kill it from your own top by pressing the k (kill) key. To exit press q (quit).

If the name of the executable is descriptive enough, we can kill it directly without searching for its pid using the Killall order:

pi @ raspberrypi: ~ $ killall -9 cat
Raspberry Pi pi @: ~ $ ▄

But keep in mind that killall sends the signal to all processes that have the CMD field like the one indicated in the argument.

Info: We propose the following exercise. Imagine that you run the file executable that you have permission setuid to root. Due to a programming error, the program does not end. What order must you execute to kill him?

Version Control

Software, like any engineering process, is an iterative process. The programs are not made at once, but gradually, adding one thing at a time. After adding a new function, it is common to perform a reengineering process, to make the whole program simpler. In this process, it is common to generate regressions; that is, things that work stop working. How do we return to the previous situation?

The solution, obviously, is managing different versions. But managing different versions manually is a tedious and error-prone process. The correct thing is to use a version control system. In this book, we propose GIT, the same one that uses the Linux kernel, and the same that we use in the documentation and in the support software of this book.

The git order is not the easiest to use program of your new Raspberry Pi, and we will not turn this book into a book about git. We will only comment on the orders you need to update the book software. That way, you will always have the latest.

The src and doc folders of your home are two GIT repositories that contain the same as in the official repositories of github.com. They were created as indicated in the appendix that describes our Raspbian customization. When a folder is a GIT repository it contains a hidden subfolder called .git

pi @ raspberrypi: ~ $ ls -d * /. git
doc /.git src /.git
Raspberry Pi pi @: ~ $ ▄

Chapter 3 - The Peripherals of the RPI

The Elements of the RPI

The Raspberry Pi has a huge number of peripherals and will not give us time to see them all. In the following sections, we will see the fundamental concepts of the majority. On the website of the book, we will be adding information that we will incorporate into future editions of this book.

Digital Inputs and Outputs

The online version of this book incorporates an interactive timeline with the history of the Raspberry Pi. Review the evolution of the Raspberry Pi concept a bit. Initially, it looked like it was going to be a USB stick, similar to the media centers that plug directly into the TV. If the goal was to reduce cost, why did it end up being much bigger?

We have to look for the answer in the objectives of the project. Its designers wanted it to be a teaching platform, not simply a cheap computer. They wanted high school students to experience for themselves not only the programming, but the construction of their own electronic equipment. It was essential that it be easy to connect things.

Therefore, from the first model, the Raspberry Pi has a good number of pins that can be configured as digital inputs or outputs to control any peripheral, sensor, or external actuator. transitions is the GPIO (General Purpose Input / Output) pins. In this chapter, we will discuss its general characteristics, and then we will see the programming details.

Comparison of the I / O Pins for the Original Models and the A + And B + Models

GPIO Connector

The original models feature a 2x13 pin connector labeled P1. All later models are compatible with these first 26 pins. This is the only one really intended to provide general purpose digital inputs and outputs. The P1 connector provides access to 17 GPIO pins. In revision 2 of the Raspberry Pi model B, next to P1 is an unpopulated socket, the 2-pin P5, which provides access to 4 additional GPIO pins.

The A + and B + models greatly extend the number of available pins from the 26-pin P1 connector to a new J8 40-pin connector. Among them, 9 more GPIO pins. However, the compatibility is total, since the first 26 pins maintain their original function.

P1 and P5 of models A and B revision 2.

Configuration of the I/O Pins in The Sockets

Digital Inputs and Outputs

From now on, we will use the numbering corresponding to the new 40-pin connector. Its equivalent in connectors P1 and P5 can be seen in the table at the beginning of this chapter. When we talk about pin numbers, we will refer to the new J8 connector unless otherwise indicated.

On the one hand, most of the pins are general purpose digital inputs / outputs. They can be configured as inputs or outputs, can be read, or written with a digital value, high or low, one or zero. Keep in mind that the high level is 3.3V, and they are not tolerant of 5V voltages.

Pins 8 and 10 can be configured as a UART interface for a conventional serial port. In fact, this is your default setting in Raspbian since the UART is used as a console.

On the other hand, pins 3 and 5 can be configured as an I2C interface to interact with peripherals that follow this protocol. In the book, we have already configured it this way. Pin 12 can be configured as PWM output. In theory, pins 12 and 13 can also be configured as an I2S (digital audio) interface, but pins are not readily available. Pins 19, 21, 23, 24 and 26 can be configured as the first interface

SPI (SPI0) to interact with peripherals that follow this protocol. In the book, we have already configured them in this way. Pins 27 and 28 are not available. They are reserved for optional incorporation of a serial memory in the expansion plates according to the HAT specification. They are the only pins that are configured as outputs at startup, and all others are initially configured as inputs to avoid problems.

Pins 29, 31, 32, 33, 35, 36, 37, 38 and 40 provide access to new GPIO legs that were not available in the original models. These legs may have other additional uses. For example, pins 32, 33, and 35 can be used for PWM outputs (only two channels available). Further, these legs complete the necessary pins to configure another SPI interface (SPI1), which we will not use in the book.

Warning

The P5 socket of the original models is originally designed to be populated from the bottom layer of the circuit. The pins in the attached figure are listed according to this criterion. If it is mounted in the upper layer, the pin assignment will be its specular reflection.

In total, we have 26 pins for digital inputs and outputs, and two of them can be used for PWM control.

GPIO Protection

When using GPIO pins for interface with hardware of any kind, care must be taken not to damage Raspberry Pi itself. It is very important to check the voltage levels and the requested current. GPIO pins can generate and consume voltages compatible with 3.3V circuits (not 5V tolerant) and can output up to 16 mA. That's enough to illuminate an LED, but for little else.

However, keep in mind that the current coming from these pins comes from the 3.3V power supply, and this source is designed for a peak load of about 3 mA for each GPIO pin. That is, even if the Broadcom SoC allows to drain up to 16 mA for each pin, the source will not be able to give more than about 78 mA in total (51 mA in the original models). There is no risk if you try to exceed this limit, but it will not work.

Warning

The GPIO pins of the Raspberry Pi are not tolerant of 5V voltages. They are intended for use with 3.3V circuits and do not have any protection. You should not drain more than 16mA per pin.

To avoid problems, a wide variety of expansion cards have been manufactured, which protect GPIO pins in various ways. The best known are:

Pi-Face Digital

Gertboard by Gert van Loo, one of the first volunteers of the Raspberry Pi Foundation. A wide variety of protection methods is available in the elinux.org tutorial titled GPIO Protection Circuits.

Program Digital Inputs and Outputs

The definitive reference for programming any of the BCM2835 peripherals is the manufacturer's data sheet, although it is a dense and arid document. The document by Gert van Loo GPIO pads control is also illustrative.

In later chapters, we will see some examples to familiarize ourselves with this peripheral, but you may want to expand the information. To begin with, probably the best tutorial is that of elinux.org, which is entitled RPi Tutorial: Easy GPIO Hardware & Software and especially programming examples using various languages and mechanisms. The Gertboard book also has abundant information, but the software is hard to find.

From the point of view of the programmer, the GPIO pins of the Raspberry Pi look like memory mapped devices. That is, to configure the pins, take digital values, or read digital signals, we have to read or write in certain memory locations. However, the Raspberry Pi processor uses a mechanism called virtual memory, in which each process sees a different address space, which does not necessarily have to correspond to the physical space, and that guarantees isolation between processes. In GNU / Linux to be able to access certain physical addresses, it is necessary to use a device (/ dev / mem) that for all purposes behaves

As a normal file. For example, in the 0x20200034 position of the device / dev / mem, the value of the GPIO0 to GPIO31 inputs can be read.

Obviously, accessing the entire physical address space is very dangerous, since it allows the entire address space of the other processes to be accessed from one process. Not only the isolation between processes is compromised, but also the security of the system. A malicious process could use privileged functions. If you think that doesn't affect you, you don't know enough about computer security. From time to time, take a look at Blackhat's presentations to see what is happening in the world of security, and you will see that it affects everything (robots, medical equipment, televisions, industrial equipment, home automation, telecommunication systems,...). A malicious user could even physically damage the Raspberry Pi. For this reason, the device / dev / mem has write permissions only for the superuser.

Recent versions of Raspbian have a / dev / gpiomem device that allows access to the GPIO pin address range only and has write permission for the gpio group. The user pi is from the gpio group. Therefore, the Pi user programs can act on GPIO pins. In practice, this may not be the case because many libraries do not yet use / dev / gpiomem.

GPIO Pin Characteristics

The GPIO pins of the Raspberry Pi incorporate a set of very interesting features:
They have the ability to limit the slew rate. This would improve noise immunity and reduce crosstalk noise, but at the cost of extending propagation times. You can program your strength drive, that is, its ability to deliver current, between 2 mA and 16 mA in 2 mA jumps (eight possible values). It basically consists of the possibility of activating more or less drivers in parallel.

For more details, consult the Gert van Loo document referred to above. Normally at startup, it is set to 8 mA. This does not mean that we cannot ask for more current. Up to 16 mA is safe. However, if we exceed 8 mA, the voltage will drop to the point that a logical one can stop being interpreted as one, and the heat dissipation will be greater. On the other hand, if we program the pins to their maximum capacity, we will have current peaks that affect consumption and may affect the operation of the microSD card, especially with capacitive loads. This effect is more noticeable, the greater the number of outputs switch simultaneously.

It is possible to configure the inputs with or without Schmitt trigger so that the low- and high-level transitions have different thresholds. This allows some noise tolerance. It is possible to enable a pullup and / or pulldown resistor. Its value is around 50KOhm.

The limitation setting of slew rate, drive strength, and input with Schmitt trigger is not done pin to pin but in blocks (GPIO0-27, GPIO28-45, GPIO46-53). For the interests of the book, there should be no problems with the default configuration.

The Physical column contains the pin number on connector J8, and column V contains the read value. The Name column represents the function of the pin, but you must be careful because when GPIO appears.21, it does not refer to the Broadcom nomenclature, which is the usual one, but to a nomenclature of the WiringPi library. To interpret it correctly, you must look at the corresponding number in the BCM column, so GPIO.21 is actually GPIO 5. This artificial confusion has been the subject of numerous criticisms to the WiringPi library, but it seems that Arduino users see it as something natural.

Alternative Functions

All GPIO pins have the possibility of being used with other alternative functions. Each GPIO pin can be configured as input, output, or as one of the six alternative functions (from Alt0 to Alt5).

Together with your book starter kit, you will receive a card that summarizes the functions that interest us. For more details, consult the flyer that we also provide you or the elinux.org documentation that includes all the scattered information. If you do not find examples of any of the peripherals and you cannot make it work, ask in the book forum.

This scheme may be useful for advanced uses:

However, you should keep in mind that some elements cannot be selected safely because they have already been used in other parts of the Raspberry Pi. For example, the BCM2837 has two SD interfaces and two UARTs. However, both SD interfaces are busy (one for the microSD card and one for WiFi communication. Similarly, UART0 is assigned to the Bluetooth interface on the Raspberry Pi 4, and only UART1 is shown on pins 8 and 10. Another example is the clocks of general purpose (GPCLKx) that allow us to generate programmable frequency clocks on certain legs.GPCLK1 is reserved for internal use (Ethernet), and if you try to use it, most likely to hang the Raspberry Pi. Nothing serious, but not pleasant either.

Manipulating Pins in the Console

We will start using the components without writing a line of code, using programs that you have available. Connect an LED to one of the legs (for example, GPIO18) with a resistor to limit the current to 15mA. For this, you can help yourself with this table taken from theledlight.com by correcting the value for the Banggood LEDs that we have in the kit.

Kind	Drop	Resistance (15mA)
Red	1.7V	100 Ohm
Yellow	2V	87 Ohm
Green	2.1V	80 Ohm
White	2.7V	40 Ohm
Blue	2.9V	27 Ohm

The kit has a set of discrete components that includes LEDs and resistors. In theory, three of each of the colors red, yellow, green, and white are included. In practice, depending on availability, they can include other types of LEDs and even another number. For example, in a test order we made at the beginning of the year, we received 15 LEDs (5 red, 5 yellow, and 5 blue). The objectives of the book are not affected at all, so this seems a minor anecdote.

The kit LEDs are not colored, so it is difficult to know what color they are. In the bags, they usually have a letter (R, G, Y, W) to indicate the color, but not always. Anyway, if we put a resistance of 100 Ohm, we are sure not to exceed the limits, and it turns on smoothly until the blue LED. Let's see how to turn on and off the connected LED to GPIO18 leg:

```
pi @ raspberrypi: ~ $ gpio -g mode 18 out
pi @ raspberrypi: ~ $ gpio -g write 18 1
pi @ raspberrypi: ~ $ gpio -g write 18 0
Raspberry Pi pi @: ~ $ ▄
```

In the first line, we have configured the leg as output. In the following, we simply write a value on that leg (1 and 0). The -g option tells gpio to use normal leg numbering.

Note: We are in luck in the Banggood kit because white diodes have a moderate voltage drop. Unfortunately, on many other occasions, this is not the case, and it is common to have 3.4V voltage drops on a white LED. A consequence of this is that we cannot turn them on with 3.3V outputs. In those cases, you can use the level shifter or a transistor, but is it necessary? Here is the challenge, if you had a white LED with a 3.4V drop, what would you do? Use the same components as before but set the circuit to turn on without problems with a GPIO leg.

The next step is to use the GPIO legs as digital inputs. To do this, connect one of the buttons between another GPIO leg and the ground. It is also normal to put a 10K pull-up resistor between the leg and 3.3V so that the input is not floating while the button is not pressed. You can do it, but we remind you that you can also use the internal pull-up.

```
pi @ raspberrypi: ~ $ gpio -g mode 23 in
pi @ raspberrypi: ~ $ gpio -g mode 23 up
pi @ raspberrypi: ~ $ gpio -g read 23
Raspberry Pi pi @: ~ $ ▂
```

Each time we run gpio -g read 23, it   will return the status (0 for the switch pressed and 1 for not pressed).

Pulse Width Modulation

Pulse Width Modulation (PWM) is a technique that consists of varying the duty cycle of a periodic digital signal, mainly with two possible objectives:

On the one hand, it can be used as a mechanism to transmit information. For example, servo motors have a digital input through which the desired angle encoded in PWM is transmitted.

On the other hand, it can be used to regulate the amount of power supplied to the load. For example, LED luminaires frequently use PWM regulators to allow intensity control.

The Raspberry Pi has several GPIO legs (GPIO12, GPIO13, GPIO18, and GPIO19) that can be configured as the output of one of the two PWM channels. BCM2835 itself is responsible for managing the signal generation, completely freeing the main processor.

The PWM peripheral of the Raspberry Pi is very flexible but only has two channels (PWM0 and PWM1). It can work in PWM mode or serializer mode. In serializer mode, simply remove the bits of the words written in a buffer in the corresponding leg. Let's look first at the PWM mode.

The user can configure two values:
- A range of values available (up to 1024).
- A value that determines the duty cycle. The PWM module is responsible for maintaining the duty cycle in the value / range ratio.

The base frequency for PWM in Raspberry Pi is 19.2Mhz. This frequency can be divided by using a divider indicated with pwmSetClock, up to a maximum of 4095. At this frequency the internal algorithm that generates the pulse sequence, but in the case of the BCM2835 there are two operating modes, a balanced mode in which it is difficult to control the width of the pulses, but allows a very high frequency PWM control, and a mark and space mode that is much more intuitive and more appropriate to control servos. The balanced mode is appropriate to control the power supplied to the load.

In mark and space mode, the PWM module will increase an internal counter until it reaches a configurable limit, the PWM range, which can be a maximum of 1024. At the beginning of the cycle, the pin will be set to 1 logical and will remain until the internal counter reaches the value set by the user. At that time, the pin will be set to 0 logical and will remain until the end of the cycle.

Let's see its application to the control of a servomotor. A servomotor has a signal input to indicate the desired inclination. Every 20ms expect a pulse, and the width of this pulse determines the inclination of the servo. Around 1.5ms is the pulse width necessary for the centered position. A smaller width rotates the servo counterclockwise (up to approximately 1ms), and a longer duration makes it rotate clockwise (up to approximately 2ms). In this case, the range and the divisor must be calculated so that the pulse is produced every 20ms, and the control of the pulse width around 1.5ms is with the maximum possible resolution.

The red servo cable (V +) is connected to + 5V in P1-2 or P1-4, the black or brown cable (V-) to GND in P1-6, and the yellow, orange, or white (signal) cable to GPIO18 on P1-12. No other components are needed.

Mounting a microservo to be controlled directly from GPIO18 configured as PWM output. To have maximum control of the servo position, we will test with the maximum range of 1024. In that case, the divisor must be such that the frequency of the PWM pulse is:

f = base
f = 19.2 × 10 6 Hz = 50 Hz
range × div
1024 × div
20 ms

That is, the splitter should be set to 390. The full range of the servo depends on the specific model. Theoretically, it should be between 52 and 102, the value being completely centered 77. In practice, the specific servo must be tested because the limits of 1ms and 2ms are not strict. Our experiments give a useful range between 29 and 123 for the TowerPro microservo available in the student kit.

Warning: Remember that there are only two PWM channels available and that these channels can only be assigned to certain legs (PWM0 in GPIO12 and GPIO18, PWM1 in GPIO13 and GPIO19).

More About PWM

For the purposes of the book, we will not stop at the PWM module, but keep in mind that the range of possibilities is much greater. We do not rule out incorporating this section in the future more information about the other modes of operation. For now, we prefer to move forward to meet other peripherals.

Keep in mind that the analog audio included in the Raspberry Pi uses the two PWM channels, so if you use analog sound, try to avoid using PWM. Our recommendation is that you use a Bluetooth speaker, or you can use an external audio board (HiFi-Berry, for example).

Configuring Raspberry Pi

To initialize our Raspberry Pi, you need to connect the peripherals you will use to the Raspberry (the essential are the SD card and the monitor); plug it in also to a power source. At startup, a screen with various information is loaded, and from there, Raspbian will be being loaded. The first time it boots up, Raspberry will display the raspiconfig tool. In case you need to run setup again, type at the command line: sudo raspi-config. Program options allow you to make the following changes:

Expand_rootfs: Allows you to expand the system of files so that you can use all of the SD card capacity.

Overscan: When a high-quality monitor is used definition, there is a possibility that the text may exceed sides of the screen, misaligning the display and losing part of the image. To correct this problem, enable the Overscan and change the values so that the image is aligned to the screen. Use positive values when the screen exit and negative values if black edges appear around it.

Configure_keyboard: The keyboard comes pre-configured with the British (UK) layout. If you want to change, select another one according to the language you will use.

Change_pass: Allows you to change the password and user.

Change_locale: Pi comes configured with the location of the United Kingdom using its style of UTF-8 encoding (en_GB.UTF-8). Select the country of your location. Example: Brazil UTF-8 (en.UTF-8).

Chang_timezone: For time zone setting, Select your region and city from your location.
Memory_split: Allows you to change the amount of memory that the GPU (graphics unit) and the CPU will use. Leave this option as default.

SSH: Allows you to enable the option to access Pi via SSH (Secure Shell) remotely over the network. Leave This option disabled allows you to save resources.

Boot Behavior: This option allows you to skip typing username and password at startup (by selecting YES). If you leave NO, you must enter these three commands (login and password can be changed in the previous option Change_pass): Raspberrypi login: pi Password: raspberry pi @ raspberrypi ~ $ startx

Update: This option allows you to update some utilities automatically, being connected to the Internet. When you have finished your settings, use the TAB key, and select Finish. It may happen that the OS restarts alone. If this does not happen and it is the first boot, type the command: pi @ raspberrypi ~ $

sudo reboot. This will force initialization with the new settings. At the desktop, we already found the Scratch programming tools and Python, in addition to the Midori browser and LXTerminal, which will be covered throughout the book.

Turning off Your Raspberry Pi (Shutting Down)

The Raspberry Pi does not have a power switch. For turn it off we should use the Logout button in the bottom corner screen right or by running the following command in shell22: pi @ raspberrypi ~ $ sudo shutdown –h now Disconnect your Pi correctly, because if pull the plug from the socket, the SD card can be corrupted and stop working.

Using Shell

Raspbian, like all Linux distribution OSs, uses the shell to execute the installation commands, modification, removal of programs, etc. The program that will be providing shell access is LXTerminal. The shell stores a command history that can be Very useful for easy typing. For example, you just need to start typing a command and hit the TAB key for the rest of the command to appear: this is very useful when you are looking for a directory. Another important facility is to be able to return the commands entered: if the execution of a command has given an error, simply press the arrow key to up, and the previous command will reappear; must then correct just the wrong part and hit enter. Previous Commands can be repeated just using the keys: up arrow, down arrow, and enter.

Let's start our programming practice. We will develop three projects with increasing levels of complexity so that you can gain expertise and develop new and increasingly sophisticated projects. You can also check out millions of examples on the

Scratch website (https://scratch.mit.edu/), as well as publish your creations.

Application Development - Easy Level

Our first project, which we classify as "easy", will be called "Labyrinth". The player's goal is to pass through the maze until they reach the portal (Labyrinth Finish Line). The player also cannot circumvent the game by hacking. If he touches the wall of the maze, he must go back and choose another direction. When the actor reaches the exit, the time taken to make the route will be shown. We started by running the Scratch application, which is on the desktop. We can start by setting the stage, which will be a maze. The stage is the background where the characters move. To assemble it, you can draw the environment or import some ready-made images. To import, you can do the following:

- In the lower left corner, click on "Load Scenario Lay Programming with Raspberry Pi from File";
- In the window that opens, make the desired file path, click on it. You can also use a library image;

In this case, use the Stage icon and select one of the options presented. In our case, we will draw a maze. The ball will travel several paths within the maze and should reach the opening. To do this, go to the bottom left corner; click the Paint New Scenery icon.

In the drawing area that opens to the right, use the Rectangle and Line drawing tools and, using your creativity, draw the maze.

Do not forget that the maze must present at least one valid path that the ball must follow, starting at a starting point (in) and ending at an ending point (out). If you want to save the stage

48

image, just go to the presentation screen and right-click, and select the "Save Picture of Stage" option. With the stage created, we can create the character that will pass through the maze; we can draw it or import it from the library, just as we did for the stage. Since we learned how to draw while setting the stage, let's now import an image from the library. To do this, go to the bottom left corner, in the Actors, New Actor area, click on the "Choose Library Actor" icon.

The library is very rich: has several character types separated by Category, Theme, and Type. Select the character you want to continue the game and click Ok. With the new Actor created, we can assign you the roles. To do this, select the actor and, in the upper strip of the screen, choose the Routes (or Scripts) option. In this tab, there is a set of commands that are separated by functions: Motion, Control, Sensors, Appearance, etc. Click the Events function, select the command When clicked, and drag it to the center of the screen: each time the "Green Flag" button is pressed, the other commands of the program will be executed.

In the following steps, we will explain the game instructions, ask the user name, create a timer, and the character control commands. Let's start by setting the character's starting position on the stage: click the Motion function, drag the Go to x: ... y: ... instruction and change the values of x and y. The x: -214 y: 160 positions correspond to the upper left side of the stage. The position of each character is always given by a pair of coordinates (x, y). To change x and y values, simply drag the object across the stage; as it is dragged, the object's coordinates (x, y) can be seen on the right of the screen. To show the game instructions, still in the Routes tab, click the Appearance function; then drag the Say statement and write the instructions to the player. To ask the player's name, click on the Sensors function and drag the Ask ... instruction and wait for the answer; you can write something else instead of what's your name?

49

- Click the Appearance function again and drag the Say ... statement for ... seconds;
- You can change the text Hello and the time. Again, go to the Appearance function and drag the Say ... command for ... seconds;
- Now go to the sensors function and drag the answer command into the Say ... command for ... seconds;

Through these commanders, the actor will return the name that was entered at the beginning of the game. We will again position our character to the x: -214 y: 160 position so that the player does not move the character while displaying the game instructions. At this point, the timer must be reset to start counting for a new game: click on the Sensors function and drag the Zero timer instruction.

At the end of the game, a message will appear with the elapsed time. The actor's initial positioning command should also be repeated, as the player may have moved the object while reading the instructions. The actor must be positioned at the beginning of the valid path to the maze. As a good observer, you may have already noticed that the commands are colorful and that they use them. This makes it easy to see a large script ready and to know which part of the function menu the commands were taken from.

Now let's work on the character's movements: walking will be the only action he has done. Since we want him to walk continuously until he can get out, click on his picture, then click on the Control function and drag the Always statement. Now we will define the condition for our character to move inside the stage, so go to the control function and drag the If statement;

Now we will define which key will move the character right, left, up, and down. Go to the Sensors function and choose the instruction key ... pressed and choose the key that will use to move your character to the left side; we use the left arrow key. With our first side defined, we will say which direction belongs on the left side. Go to the Motion function and drag the instruction point to the direction and position the direction that belongs to the left side, in this case - 90 degrees. Select the Routes tab again, click on the Motion function; drag the Move ... steps instruction into the always opening;

In this command, we define that the character will walk when we press one of the arrows; type 5 in the number of steps. Repeat for the remaining three directions. To advance the process and not have to type the entire command again by hand, go to the first code and click the right button and choose the duplicate option so you can duplicate the code and change it without having to rewrite the code.

When the character touches the walls of the maze, he must return (the player cannot cheat through a wall). For this, we need to use decision and repeat commands: when touching the maze line, he must go back 5 steps to be within the allowed limits. To use decision commands, click the Sensors function and drag the instruction Tapping color ...?;

Then click on the color box and select the desired color from the color box that appears. The mouse cursor will cause the color box to change according to the color it passes over. Now let's create the maze output:

- We draw a portal;
- When the cat touches him, the game will be over, and the victory song will be played.

The portal must be an actor. Since we already imported an actor from the library, in this case, we will draw him. In the lower left corner of the screen, under Actors, New Actor, click Paint New Actor (Brush icon). Now use your creativity and draw the portal. With the portal created, let's put its functions. The new actor's first command is the same as that used for the first actor: clicking on the green start flag (Events) and positioning yourself (Movement); The portal should be positioned in the final exit position of the maze. The next command will be Control (the Always Repeat). The next command defines the end of the game: every time our character (Cat) touches the Portal, the message of victory will be given, the time with which the course was made, and a song will be played. Try to complete the script: the commands exit the Events, Motion, Control, Sensors, Sound, Appearance, and Control again.

We have already seen that we can put sounds in the project: from the library, importing a sound of our own or recording a sound. We even saw that we have resources to edit the sounds that we will use. Let's put the sound in our project by importing it from the library. Select the Sound function and drag the Play Sound ... command. Now click on the Sounds tab; then click on the Upload sound from file icon, scroll to the Scratch library path and select the Congratulations sound. This concludes the first project. Note the start and end points. To play, click on the green flag and use the arrow keys to command the character.

Application Development - Middle Level

Now let's create a Ping Pong game to play in pairs, which we can consider at an intermediate level. This project is very interesting because it works with practically all functions of the Scratch platform. The goal of the game is also simple: whoever can play the ball beyond the opponent's racket score points; who can make 5 points, is the winner. First, let's create the stage: it will have two lines behind the rackets, representing the limit to how far the ball will reach; whenever the ball touches these lines, the point will be the opponents. Following the script and draw the stage. The red and blue colors are important as they will be used as a control to score points for each player. The ball to use in the game is an actor; let's import it from the library. Now let's create the rackets;

Just create one and then duplicate it. Go to the Actors area (bottom left) and click the Paint New Actor (brush) icon. To duplicate the racket, in the Actors area, right-click it; in the popup menu, click Duplicate. The duplicate option creates a new character in the Actor area. The second racket will have no link to the first racket. Drag the rackets and scoreboard (Player 1 Player 2 variables) across the stage. Once the stage and the characters are created, we will program the ball and then the balls and rackets. At the beginning of the game, the ball should be in the center of the stage. Enter the commands:

When you click and Go to x: ... and y: ... and type 0 for x and y. Then drag the Point instruction to the direction 90 degrees (from the Motion function); click on the box to enter the degrees (90) and within that command, go to the Operators function and drag the command Choose a number between 1 and 10; enter 180 instead of 10. Now let's set the score for two players (there will be two variables). To do this, select the Variables function, click Create a variable, and type Player 1; do the same for Player 2. Remember that variables will only be created for the ping pong ball, they will serve as a counter for the game score. Leave the two checkboxes next to the variables checked so that they appear on the Stage; drag them on the Stage to place them in the position you want.

The two variables (representing each player's score) must start the game with zero. To do so, double-drag the command change Player to 0 for the script; change the first instruction to Player 1 and to 0 (zero); change the second statement to Player 2 and to 0 (zero). Also, drag the instruction wait 1 sec from the Control function and change the time to 1.5 seconds.

Score Counting Variables

The game should last until one of the players (Player 1 or Player2) reaches 5 points. To do this, drag the command Repeat until it is in the Control functions. There is a hexagon after the until: drag the operator or to the hex (also from the Control function); now, we have two hexagons.

Drag the = operator to the first hexagon. To the first box of or drag Player 1 (from the Variables function); in the second box, type 5. Repeat for Player 2: drag the = operator to the second hex; to the first box or drag Player 2 (from the Variables function); In the second box, type 5.

Decision Commands

Within the Command, repeat until most of the project logic occurs. The ball should come back every time it touches the edge;

If we do not put this command, the ball will be stuck on the edge without returning to the game. To do this, drag to the opening of Repeat until the command. If you touch the edge, come back (from the Motion function): this is a decision command that performs a single statement: back. The following instruction Move 7 steps (also from the Motion function) will always be executed even if the ball does not touch the border. Drag the If ... Then statement (from the Control function); drag the instruction Touching color? to the hexagon; put the black color in the box. To select the color inside the canister, click on the color inside the canister and drag the mouse to the black color. Touching the black color, the ball should come back. To program this, do the following: drag the Point instruction to the direction ... degrees (Motion function); then drag the minus operator (Operators function) to the ellipse with the degree value (we now have two ellipses to fill in); to the first ellipse, drag the direction instruction (from the Motion function); at the second ellipse type 180. We want the ball to make a random move on the way back so that its trajectory becomes unpredictable, and the game gets busier. Drag the instruction rotate ... degrees (from the Motion function); then drag the Pick number operator between ... and ... (from the Operators function); type - 20 in the first ellipse and 20 in the second. Next, we want the ball to move in that direction: drag the Move ... steps instruction (Motion function) and type 10 in the ellipse. If the ball touches the edge of the stage, we should score the opponent and return the ball to the center of the stage.

To do this, drag the If ... Then and Tapping Color ... commands; put the color blue. This command should be just below the Se, still inside Repeat until. Now drag the Add to ... statement (from the Variables function) into the opening of the If ... then; select Player 1 for the variable to add. Drag instruction Wait ... sec (Control function); type 2 for seconds. Drag Go to x: ... y: ... (Motion function) and type 0 for both. The instructions for counting Player 2 are almost identical. Repeat, therefore, the steps of the previous paragraph, changing only the player and the color. When either Player 1 or Player 2 reaches 5 points, the program will exit the Repeat command until that is what this command controls. Then we need to see who made the 5 points. To do so, drag another If ... statement then ... (from the Control function) to after the Repeat command until. Drag to the hexagon of If ... the operator = (from the Operators function); to the first box do = drag Player 1 (from the Variables function); in the second box, type 5. Now drag to the first opening of the Se ... then, otherwise ... the Say ... statement for ... seconds; type in "Player 1 Champion !!!" and 2 in the seconds box.

Right-click this instruction, and on the popup menu, click Duplicate. Drag the duplicate statement to the Snag opening and click again to drop the copied statement; type "Player 2" in place of "Player 1". These are the commands defined for the ball actor. Since we have three actors on stage (the ball and two rackets), we need to write the racket scripts. Rackets can only move up and down. The first will use the W keys to go up and S to go down; the second will use the up arrow and down arrow keys. We need two command blocks for each racket. Have you seen the commands When you click and Go to x: ... y: ... and the Always command. The command set then programs the racket to go up when you press the W key. To the hexagon drag the Command key ... pressed (from the Sensors function) and select W to the key;

inside the opening of If ... then two instructions will enter: Add ... ay (from the Motion function) and another If ... then. Enter 15 in the first statement;

This changes the position of the racket, causing it to rise as it increases the value of its y coordinate. As the racket went up, the following statement

If ... then checks if it touched the edge: drag the Tapping ... command? (from the Sensors function) to the hexagon and select edge. Drag another instruction Go to x: ... and y: ... to the second If ... then type - 42 and 11. The other instruction set programs the racket to come down when you press the S key. and check if it touched the bottom edge. You can duplicate the whole set: right-click the If ... statement and then Duplicate. Drag the duplicate statement below If ..., then still inside Always, and click to drop it. Make the appropriate changes: Select Y instead of W; enter -15 in place 15; type -293 instead of 11. Note that by keeping the x value constant at -42 and varying y, the racket only moves vertically (up and down). For Player 2, the only changes are: Up Arrow and Down Arrow keys and racket x and y positions. Since the instruction group looks similar, you can duplicate it.

Right-click the instruction. When you click ... and select Duplicate: The entire group of "docked" statements will be duplicated. Drag the instruction group into the Actors area and click to drop it onto actor Racket 2. Now click on actor Racket 2 to have its script (the duplicate) shown. Change the keys and x and y positions.

Application Development - Hard Level

Let's now create a difficult level game that we will call Block Breaker: The Game will have a Menu, game over screen and will be controlled by the mouse. The interesting thing about the block breaking game is that it works with practically all the functions found on the Scratch platform and the player will have a lot of fun developing the game and playing, as the main objective of the game is to be able to break all the blocks in the shortest time.

Let's import the library stage: go to the bottom left corner and click on the Choose background icon;

Several models of the library are shown, choose one (this may be Brick wall 1) and click Ok. Using Paint Editor (see item PAINT EDITOR) draw a green line at the bottom of the wall;

Note that there is a scroll bar under the stage;

Remember to draw the line along its full length.

This line will be the limit: every time the ball touches it, thus passing through the racket, a message of Game Over will be sent, and the game will end. Now let's create the racket (our first actor) that will hit the ball to break the blocks. Repeat what you have already done; the racket is now horizontal and blue. The blocks that will be destroyed by the ball are also actors. Just as you did with the racket, draw a block. Duplicate the blocks (in our case, we get 18 blocks). Name the blocks by numbering them: Block 1, Block 2, Block 3 ... and set the colors for the blocks to have a heterogeneous structure. Our other actor is the ball; let's import it from the library. After creating all the actors, drag them on the stage. Now we need to program each of these characters. The first script will be the racket: it will only walk on the x axis, following the mouse, and should hit the ball. Click on the Actor Racket, and on the Scripts, tab enter the two start instructions. When you click and Go to x: ... and y: ...; change the starting position to x: -58 and yy: -148. Then enter the Always statement.

Drag the Change x statement to ... (from the Motion function) to the Always open; then drag the Mouse Position x instruction (from the Sensors function) to the typing box. This will keep the racket on the same line (y axis) but will follow the mouse to the right and left (varying the x axis). This is just the racket script. The blocks also have a simple behavior: when the game starts, they show themselves in a certain position; if they are touched by the ball, they hide.

To do this, we will use two new commands: Show and Hide (from the Appearance function). Click on a block to start your script. Put the command When you click ... (from the Events function), then drag the Show (from the Appearance function) command and the Go to x: ... y: ... (from the Motion function) and type -186 and 176. Enter the Always statement (from the Control function) and drag, within its opening, an If ... Then statement (from the Control function); drag the instruction Tapping ...? (from the Sensors function) after Se ... and select Ball from the selection box. Inside If ... then, enter two commands: Wait ... sec (from the Control function) and Hide (from the Appearance function); enter 0.2 for seconds (duplicate the script for each block and change only the position of each).

Now let's develop the functions of the main character, the little ball. In addition to moving in any direction, the ball will also control the player's score: every time he destroys one of the blocks, it will add a point for the player. Click on the ball, in the Actors area, and on Scripts. Enter the command When you click ... (from the Events function) and o Go to x: ... y: ... (from the Motion function) and type -26 and 67. That way, the ball will be

58

above the racket. Drag the Point statement to the direction ... degrees (from the Motion function) and select 0 for the degrees; This direction makes the ball go up. In the Variables function, create a variable named Score. Drag the Change ... to ... instruction to get the score to start with zero. The game ends in three situations: if all blocks are destroyed, time is up, or if the ball touches the green line. Let's put the Always loop function; within the opening of this command. The next other command blocks will always come. Drag both instructions Move ... steps, and If you touch the border, go back (from the Motion function); This sets the speed of the ball and keeps it within the edges of the stage.

The next block will add 1 point to the scoreboard if a block is destroyed; It will take a little work because there are so many blocks. Drag the If ... Then command (from the Control function). Drag the Raspberry Pi 111 Or operator (from the Operators function) to the hex after the If. now drag to the first hex of the instruction Tapping ...? (from the Sensors function) and select Block 1. Now you need to test the other blocks. To the empty hex of the Or drag another operator Or; to the first empty hexagon drag another instruction Tapping ...? and select Block 2. To empty Or's hexagon drag another Or operator; to the first empty hexagon drag another instruction Tapping ...? and select Block 3. Since we have 18 blocks, you should repeat this process for the first 17 blocks. The last operator Or will receive in each hexagon a Tapping ...? Instruction, one for Block 17 and one for Block 18. Then we will put three commands, which will be executed when a block is destroyed: add 1 point on the scoreboard, turn the ball back and play a song. Drag the Add to ... 1 statement from the Variables function; select Score. Drag the Point statement to the direction ... degrees; complete it by placing an operator less the same as you did previously. Drag the Play Sound ... statement from the Sound function and import a song from the library.

When the ball touches the racket, it must change direction and make a random movement; We have already done this with the ping pong ball. Drag another statement If ... then; then drag the Tapping ... statement to the If hex. (from the Sensors function) and select Racket. Drag into the If ... then the Point to direction ... degrees direction; complete it by placing an operator less the same as you did; Now, however, the subtraction is reversed. Then drag the Rotate ... degrees instruction (from the Motion function) and complete it. If the ball passes the racket and touches the green line, the game ends, and the player's score is shown. You have already used them all: If ... then, with Tapping color ... Say ... for ... seconds and Stop. If the score reaches the maximum, we display the Congratulations message and the score obtained by the player. You have already used them all: If ... then; the others can be duplicated. We still have to watch the timer: let's limit the playing time to two minutes; if it exceeds, Game over! Drag another function If ... then (from the Control function); drag to hex after the If Greater operator> (from the Operators function); now drag to the first hex of the> Timer Value (from the Sensors function) statement; type 120 in the second hex of>. Duplicate the two instructions Say ... for ... seconds and Stop ... and place them inside the Se ... opening then.

Chapter 4 - I2C Communications

The Raspberry Pi has two peripherals to implement I2C, the BSC (Broadcom Serial Controller) that implements the master mode, and the BSI (Broadcom Serial Interface) that implements the slave mode. We will describe only the BSC, which has much greater interest for this book.

The BSC implements three independent masters that have to be on separate I2C buses (does not allow multi-master). However, BSC0 is reserved for the identification of expansion plates (HAT specification, pins 27 and 28), and BSC2 is exclusively for the HDMI interface. We will, therefore, usually use BSC1, using pins 3 and 5 of connector J8.

The programming interface is, as in all Raspberry Pi peripherals, a set of memory mapped records. However, in this case, there is an operating system kernel driver that significantly simplifies life.

Explore the Bus

Devices connected to an I2C bus have a 7-bit address. Although there is the possibility of using 10-bit addresses, the truth is that it is quite rare to find devices with addresses of more than 7 bits. In this book, we will assume 7-bit addresses. This implies that at most, we can have 117 devices connected (some addresses are reserved).

The first thing we can do is discover what I2C interfaces we have available. In the original models, only BSC0 was available, while in the new BS0, it is used for the identification of HAT (hardware attached on top) expansion boards. You can examine it yourself by running i2cdetect:

pi @ raspberrypi: ~ $ i2cdetect -l
I2C-1 I2C 3f804000.i2c I2C adapter Raspberry Pi pi @: ~ $ ▄
Only one I2C interface (i2c-1) appears. Now we can look at what devices are connected on the bus. Connect the MPU6050 module that is included in the kit. Just connect GND, VCC to 3.3V, SDA, and SCL. We will use i2cdetect again, indicating now the available I2C bus number:

```
pi @ raspberrypi: ~ $ i2cdetect -y 1
        012345678           9 a b c d e f
00:     - - - - - -         - - - - - - -
10:     - - - - - - - - -   - - - - - - -
twenty: - - - - - - - - -   - - - - - - -
30:     - - - - - - - - -   - - - - - - -
40:     - - - - - - - - -   - - - - - - -
fifty:  - - - - - - - - -   - - - - - - -
60:     - - - - - - - - 68  - - - - - - -
70: - - - - - - - -
Raspberry Pi pi @: ~ $ ▄
```

Only one device connected with address 68 is displayed in hexadecimal (0x68). Actually, the MPU6050 can have two addresses setting the leg AD0. Normally that little leg has a pull-down that sets it to logical zero, which corresponds to the address 0x68, but we can connect it to 3.3V to have the address 0x69. This allows to have two MPU6050 on the same bus. One with address 0x68 and one with address 0x9.

We can now read and write on any of the connected I2C devices.

We have read register 117 of the device with address 0x68 of the bus i2c -1. The MPU6050 is an accelerometer and gyroscope of InvenSense also measures temperature and can be combined directly with a magnetometer to have an IMU (Inertial Measurement Unit) complete.

If we look at the map of records, record 117 corresponds to Who Am I., and it is a record that simply returns the base address of the device. It can be used to make sure the device is in the expected direction and is responding. It is a read-only record, so if we try to write on, it will ignore it completely.

Let's read the last temperature measurement. The measurement is in registers 65 and 66, but if we read the two registers independently, we can be reading part of the temperature of one measurement and another part of another measurement. That is why you have to read the two records at once, making a 16-bit transfer (word mode):

pi @ raspberrypi: ~ $ i2cget -y 1 0x68 65 w
0x0000
Raspberry Pi pi @: ~ $ ▄

Oops, a strange value. Something fails. It is normal to take a little time to carefully read the data sheet and the map of records to understand how it works. The clue to the problem comes to us as soon as we try to read record 107 (Power Management 1):

pi @ raspberrypi: ~ $ i2cget -and 1 0x68 107
0x40
Raspberry Pi pi @: ~ $ ▄

That means that bit 6 is set to one, which curiously corresponds to the SLEEP mode. The device starts in sleep mode to not consume battery, and we have to wake it up by removing that bit.

This is something else. We already have temperature readings. But it is very important to interpret them well. I2C is a byte-oriented protocol. It is transferred byte to byte. When transferring a word through I2C, the computer understands that the low byte first arrives and then the high one. This agreement is called little-endian and is the dominant one today.

However, if we look at the map of records, we will see that address 65 corresponds to the high byte and 66 to the low byte. Therefore, the bytes are changed! The reading must be interpreted as 0xf290. Let's see how we can do it with the shell:

```
pi @ raspberrypi: ~ $ T = $ (i2cget -y 1 0x68 65 w)
pi @ raspberrypi: ~ $ echo "0x $ {T: 4: 2} $ {T: 2: 2}"
0xf230
Raspberry Pi pi @: ~ $ ▂
```

Whatever the order takes, we put it in a variable, and then we print it, followed by the two characters. It's time to think about doing a program in C or Python. But even if it is to leave the full example, we will make the complete transformation at a temperature in degrees Celsius:

```
pi @ raspberrypi: ~ $ echo "$ (($ T - 0x10000)) / 340 + 36.53"
| bc -l 26.1300000000000000000
Raspberry Pi pi @: ~ $ ▂
```

We make up the formula that comes in the map of records. The temperature is the value of the record correctly interpreted match by 340 plus 36.5. The problem is that the shell does not know how to do arithmetic operations with real ones, so we leave it to another program, in this case, bc. To bc, we pass the expression to be calculated, which is 0xf230 / 340 + 36.5. The problem is that bc does not understand hexadecimal numbers, so we have to pass it to signed decimal. This can be done with the $ ((x)) operator of the shell, which is used to calculate simple operations with integers. As it is negative, its value is the result of subtracting 0x10000.

Too complicated? Yes, I think so too. That is why we need to simplify this with the most powerful mechanism offered by computer science: abstraction. But we will leave this by the time we see how to implement all these readings in C or Python.

The i2cdump command allows a set of records to be read in a burst. We read at once from register 61 to 72. They correspond to the readings of (in order):

Accelerometer:
Acceleration in X: 0xfdf4
Acceleration in Y: 0xfe5c
Acceleration in Z: 0x3ef0
Temperature: 0xf160.
Gyroscope:
X rotation: 0xffa2
Y rotation: 0xff39
Z rotation: 0xff78

It only remains to interpret these numbers as signed integers in addition to 2. It is proposed as an exercise.

The gyroscope measures the speed of rotation in the three axes. Obviously, if a global reference is not available, error will accumulate, and its absolute measurement will not be very useful in determining the actual orientation. That is why the MPU6050 has the option of coupling with a magnetometer, which provides a real reference of the north, which allows for correcting the accumulated errors. In the book, we will not use magnetometer, but consider it for your projects.

Chapter 5 - SPI Communications

SPI is an alternative protocol to I2C that many devices use. Today it is common to find devices that implement both I2C and SPI. The choice of which one to use depends on the application:

- I2C uses fewer pins and allows to address many more devices.
- SPI uses more pins but allows much faster speed.

Like I2C, it is a serial protocol, but the address of the devices is not transmitted through the data channel, but specific legs are used to select them. As in I2C, there is a teacher who takes the active role in communication and one or several slaves who assume the passive role.

Home SPI interface has at least four legs:

- SCLK (Serial CLocK). Clock signal with respect to which the rest of the signals are synchronized.
- MISO (Master In, Slave Out). Data input for the master, data output for the slave.
- MOSI (Master Out, Slave In). Data output for the master, data input for the slave.
- CEn (Chip Enable). One or more target selection signals active at low level. To send or receive from the zero device, the signal CE0 is activated, for the device, one CE1 is activated, etc.

In the Raspberry Pi, we have three independent peripherals to implement the slave and master mode. The slave mode incorporates it into the same BSI (Broadcom Serial Interface) that also implements the I2C slave. In the book, we will see the master mode, which has much more practical interest.

The Raspberry Pi has three SPI master interfaces (SPI0, SPI1 and SPI2) although only one of them (SPI0) is visible for the original models and two of them (SPI0 and SPI1) for the models with J8 40-pin connector. Each of these interfaces has two destination selection lines (CE0 and CE1). SPI0 is more evolved since it allows DMA (direct memory access). SPI0 is designed for high-speed transfers (clock up to 125Mhz) without producing a significant load for the processor. However, SPI1 has no possibility of using DMA and only has a small four-bit 32-bit FIFO.

The student kit has an analog-digital converter with SPI interface CJMCU-1118, which incorporates the Texas Instruments ADS1118. It is a 16-bit analog-digital converter with programmable gain amplifier and with a temperature sensor. It can measure four analog signals referred to ground or two differential analog signals. We will illustrate the use of SPI with this module.

To do this, we will have to study your data sheet well before working with it. For now, to familiarize ourselves with the device, we will connect a 10K potentiometer.

Mounting a 10KOhm potentiometer as an analog source for the CJMCU-1118. To communicate with an SPI device, we must first configure a series of parameters:

The polarity of the chip select signal (CSPOL). It is normally active at a low level and does not need to be modified.

The polarity of the clock (CPOL). A value of 0 means that the rest level of the clock is low. A value of 1 means that the rest level of the clock is high.

The reloj phase (CPHA). If it has a value of 0, it means that SCLK transitions occur in half of every bit of data transmitted. A value of 1 means that SCLK transitions occur at the beginning of each bit.

Clock frequency. It is configured by selecting a clock source and a divider (CDIV). The clock source is usually 125MHz. The different combinations of CPOL and CPHA give rise to the four possible modes:

Mode	CPOL	CPHA
0	0	0
1	0	1
2	1	0
3	1	1

From the ADS1118 data sheet, we can see that the device is compatible with mode 1 (CPOL = 0, CPHA = 1). The CE polarity is also active low and supports a clock of up to 4MHz. To interact with it, we will use the tools included in the pigpio library. In particular, we will use pigpiod and its interface of pigs orders. First, we run the pigpiod server:

pi @ raspberrypi: ~ $ sudo pigpiod
Raspberry Pi pi @: ~ $ ▄

We use sudo to run with superuser permissions. It is called a server because it handles client requests. By itself, it does nothing but waits for a client to request specific operations. The client is called pigs and can run as a normal user. For example:

pi @ raspberrypi: ~ $ pigs help
...

Raspberry Pi pi @: ~ $ ▄

Countryside	Meaning
mm	SPI mode
ppp	CEi polarity. 0 = active low, 1 = active high.
uuu	Use of CEi. 0 = used, 1 = not used.
TO	Auxiliary SPI. 0 = normal SPI, 1 = auxiliary SPI.
W	Number of cables 0 = 4 wires (normal), 1 = 3 wires.
nnnn	Number of bytes to write before changing MOSI to MISO (only for W = 1).
T	Order of transmitted bits. 0 = MSb first, 1 = LSb first.
R	Order of bits received. 0 = MSb first, 1 = LSb first.
bbbbbb	Word size in bits (0-32). 0 = 8 bits. Only for auxiliary SPI.

We are lucky because most of the default parameters correspond to the values that the CJMCU-1118 module needs. Just change the SPI mode.

pi @ raspberrypi: ~ $ pigs spio 0 4000000 10
Raspberry Pi pi @: ~ $ ▄

Now, we have to configure the module with the inputs referred to ground, in continuous mode at 128 SPS and with measuring range (FSR) of ± 2,048V. The ADS1118 writes your configuration while reading data. If you don't want to write the configuration log, you just have to write zeros.

With the printf program, we can print values in a similar way to the printf C function. The $ (order) operator of the shell simply returns the standard output of the order it encloses. In this case, we use it to put the sample in hexadecimal in the variable V. We then use the operator $ ((expr)) of the shell to transform that hexadecimal number into decimal, and we compose an expression that is calculated by bc.

Chapter 6 - UART Communication

UART stands for Universal Asynchronous Receiver Transmitter. It is the dominant serial communication interface in low-end microcontrollers and old computers. Before USB, the UART was the mechanism to connect the keyboard, the mouse, or even the communications modem. Before, it was still the interface used by terminals or consoles to interact with a computer. The Terminal program that you run on your Raspberry Pi is nothing but an emulation of these old terminals.

Nowadays, it is almost impossible to find one of these serial interfaces on a computer, and it has been practically replaced by USB. Fortunately, we have special USB cables that incorporate a UART-USB adapter. In the student kit of this book, you have one. This adapter allows you to communicate the UART of the Raspberry Pi with any USB port, either from a computer or another Raspberry Pi. This allows you to use the Raspberry Pi without having a monitor and without having a network connection or USB keyboard. For example, from another Raspberry Pi or from a laptop.

The serial port occupies the GPIO14 (TxD) and GPIO15 (RxD) pins. By default, Raspbian uses these pins for a serial console. The Broadcom SoC supports two UARTs, but both are configured on the same pins of the J8 header. UART0 is a standard ARM peripheral (PL011) and implements all expected capabilities in a high performance UART. UART1 implements a simplified version that is called mini-UART by the manufacturer. It is intended to be used with low transfer rate devices, such as the console.

In all Raspberry Pi models except in the Compute Module, we only have GPIO14 and GPIO15 pins for both UARTs. For this reason, Raspbian uses UART0 for the console, and UART1 is not usually used.

But of course, that means the UART is busy on the console. It is necessary to remove the console in order to use the UART for other purposes. To disable the console, you have to edit the file /boot/cmdline.txt as superuser, delete the fragment that says console = serial0,115200, and restart the Raspberry Pi.

To use the GPIO14 and GPIO15 pins as digital input / output pins, use the configuration tool and, in the Interfaces, tab deactivate the Serial option.
But let's go back to its use as a console, which is very useful when you want to put your Raspberry Pi in a robot or other equipment where plugging a monitor is unthinkable. It is possible to connect a USB cable to these pins to connect to the Raspberry Pi without the need for any network configuration. In the student kit, you will have received a USB cable on one end and with four female Dupont connectors on the other. You can connect it in the following way:
The red wire is the USB power (5V). The Raspberry Pi already has its own power, so you must connect it again. The black wire is the ground, connect it to pin J8-6. The white cable is the data transmission from the UART to the USB port. Connect it to pin J8-8 (GPIO14).

The green cable is the one to receive data from the USB port to the UART. Connect it to pin J8-10 (GPIO15).

This should be enough to have the console running on any Raspberry Pi model before 3B. The problem is that in the Raspberry Pi 4, the UART is used for the Bluetooth interface, and the console is configured with the mini-UART. This has important consequences that are not entirely resolved yet. As a user, you are not going to face the problems it poses at all, but keep in mind that for the mini-UART to work correctly, you have to set the core frequency to 250 MHz; it is not possible to modulate the frequency to save consumption.

Testing the console is very simple, using Raspberry Pi itself. Also, connect the USB end of the cable to a free USB port and run:

pi @ raspberrypi: ~ $ miniterm.py / dev / ttyUSB0 115200
Raspbian GNU / Linux 8 raspberrypi ttyS0
raspberrypi login:

Enter as pi user and raspberry password. As you can see, you have a fully functional console in the UART. You can connect to it with any laptop and use the Raspberry Pi without the need for a monitor and keyboard.

For mobile devices, it is a great advantage. To exit miniterm.py, press the Ctrl, AltGr, and] key.

It is beyond the objectives of the book to explain how to use the console from a Windows laptop. If you have a GNU / Linux on your laptop, the system is the same, as we have explained. Install the screen tool and use it the same as we have used miniterm.py. In that case, you get out with Ctrl-A followed by \.

Chapter 7 - Network Communications

The most used Raspberry Pi models (B, B +, 2B, and 3B) incorporate an Ethernet interface. The new 3B model also incorporates a WiFi interface, and most users of other models use a USB WiFi skewer (WiFi dongle) to update the system. Therefore, it is obligatory that we speak a little of communications, although we will do it from a purely practical perspective, without going into excessively technical details. Of course, we recommend that you expand the information with the extensive literature available.

Communication networks today use the family of TCP / IP protocols for the most part. These are the protocols that were designed to build the Internet, the network of networks. There are two versions currently in use IPv4 (Internet Protocol v4) and IPv6. Although they are quite similar, there are important differences that mostly escape the interest and scope of this book. We will see enough of IPv4 to handle our communication needs between devices and leave IPv6 for future editions when their degree of adoption is higher.
The TCP / IP family of protocols is primarily built on the IP protocol, which provides basic capabilities and guarantees. These include addressing and routing.

IPv4 Addresses

Each network interface can have several IP addresses, and we can manage them if we want to manually. IP addresses basically work as postal codes. They are organized hierarchically, which facilitates delivery. For example, if we send a letter to the 45005 zip code, the mailman knows it is from Toledo because it starts with 45. Therefore, it will arrive first at the Toledo post office, which in turn will distribute it to its different provincial delegations. On the Internet, each post office is called a router, and the IP addresses, unlike postal codes, fully identify the recipient computer.

But how do messages get to a computer? A network interface is clearly needed. Therefore, the addresses are associated with that network interface. It can be understood as a door of a house. The mailman leaves the letter at a door, but nothing prevents a house from having more than one door. Each door has a different address (number) associated.

Let's examine a little the network of my own Raspberry Pi, and then we will see how to configure yours. We are interested in the last part of the output of the ip addr command, which can also be achieved like this:

pi @ raspberrypi: ~ $ ip addr list wlan0

3: wlan0: < BROADCAST, MULTICAST, UP, LOWER_UP > mtu 1500 qdisc mq state UP group default qlen 1000 link / ether 00: 13: ef: 71: 03: d0 brd ff: ff: ff: ff: ff: ff inet 192.168.1.38/24 brd 192.168.1.255 global scope wlan0 valid_lft forever preferred_lft forever inet6 fe80:: 146d: 4f11: 30bf: 17a4 / 64 scope link valid_lft forever preferred_lft forever
Raspberry Pi pi @: ~ $ ▪

Three address lists appear: link / ether correspond to what is known as link level addresses. It is a very important technical term, but that we will not see in the book. The inet tag corresponds to the IPv4 data, which we will use in the book. The inet6 tag corresponds to the IPv6 data that we will leave for future extensions. Let's stop on the IPv4 data.

The IP address (e.g., 192.168.1.38) is a sequence of 4 octets (numbers 0 to 255), usually separated by periods. The suffix / 24 serves to indicate which part of the address (in bits counted from the most significant) is common to all the subnet and what part is specific to each computer in the subnet. With the metaphor of the mail, it would be equivalent to determining which part of the address is the name of the street and which part is the house number. In our case, 192.168.1 is common for the entire network, and only the last number is indicative of the computer.

The scope or scope of the address indicates in which contexts that address makes sense. The interesting addresses have global reach, allow to communicate to the computer with any of those connected to the entire Internet. Other addresses will have host scope, as with the lo interface. These addresses are not intended to communicate processes beyond your computer, and it would be a mistake to pretend to use it to communicate two different computers.

Name Service

And it doesn't surprise you that after all these years using the Internet you never had to use IP addresses? Well, maybe in the configuration of the WiFi hotspot, or to share files between mobiles, but little else. I'm wrong?

The reason is that this address mechanism is simplified with another additional protocol, the name service (DNS, Domain Name System). It is a service similar to the yellow pages of the phones. We don't have to know or remember all the phones; we just have to look for the name in the phone book. The DNS works similarly.

Transport Protocols

A communications network is here to communicate, so let's do it. In this chapter, we will only use tools from your Raspberry Pi without typing a single line of programs. We will start with netcat, a wonderful tool to test network programs. Open two different terminals and execute the following in the first one:

pi @ raspberrypi: ~ $ nc -l 8888

The program waits (option l means listen, listen) without doing anything. It is what is known as a server. Go to the other terminal and execute the following.

pi @ raspberrypi: ~ $ nc 127.0.0.1 8888

Message Test

This time we run netcat as a client connected to address 127.0.0.1. That is the address of the loopback interface, so we connect to our own computer. Look in the first terminal. Magic! Type now in the first terminal:

pi @ raspberrypi: ~ $ nc -l 8888
Message Test

Another Message Test

It looks like that? You have a bidirectional data channel. You can send and receive interchangeably. To exit press the key Ctrl and without releasing press the letter C.

The number 8888 is what is known as a port number. If we continue with the post metaphor, it would be equivalent to the mailbox inside an apartment house. A port is reserved for each service. Ports below 1024 are privileged in the sense that they are used for system services and therefore a normal user cannot handle requests on those ports. Let's look at an example, port 80 is the web server port. Run this:

pi @ raspberrypi: ~ $ sudo ip addr add 161.67.137.169 dev lo
pi @ raspberrypi: ~ $ sudo nc -l 80 << EOF

HTTP / 1.0 200 OK
< html > < body > < h1 > You fool! </ h1 > </ body > </ html
>

EOF

Now run the web browser and try to view the page www.uclm.es. Surprised?
We have added an IP address to the interface loopback that matches that of www.uclm.es. When we enter this site in the browser, it uses the DNS to obtain the corresponding IP address and sends a request message to that IP address. As it is a known IP address, the message does not even leave the computer; it remains the loopback interface. In all directions of the computer, we have netcat listening on port 80, so that message request comes to netcat. What is between and EOF is just a way of indicating that this is what you should write by standard input. And what is written by standard netcat input is responsible for sending it to the other end of the communication. Voilà! A poor web server.

This example will have made it clear to you why IP addresses can only be set by the system administrator. Otherwise, it would be trivial to make man-in-the-middle attacks against the users of that computer. I think you can delete that address from the loopback interface.

pi @ raspberrypi: ~ $ sudo ip addr of 161.67.137.169 dev lo
Raspberry Pi pi @: ~ $ ▂

You already know how to communicate data, but not only between two terminals of the same computer. If you are connected to the network, try connecting the two netcat by running each one on a different computer. You already know how to communicate data with TCP / IP!

Chapter 8 - Transmission Control Protocol

Internet is much more hostile than you can see with a test on your own Raspberry Pi. Communications between computers that are more than ten thousand kilometers away involve dozens of intermediate devices. There is a negligible probability that something is not going well. Message losses or even network reorganizations are normal during the same communication process. What should you do then? The answer is both simple and comforting: nothing. What can be done is already done by the underlying protocol, TCP (Transmission Control Protocol). When you used netcat, you were using TCP without knowing it. It is a transport protocol built on IP. This protocol provides mechanisms for flow control, fragmentation, reassembly, data integrity, reordering, and retransmission so that the communication experience is as close as possible to the ideal, even if things are not going well. It is so important that the entire family of Internet protocols is called TCP / IP, although TCP and IP are only two protocols in the family.

There is no doubt that he has succeeded. The vast majority of large-scale Internet services are built on TCP: the web, email, instant messaging systems, the directory service, and virtually everything that requires end-to-end encryption.

However, to provide TCP delivery guarantees, you have to use a series of time-consuming mechanisms, and it is a time that is not easily controllable. It is said that TCP introduces unbounded latency. That is, it is not possible to quantify exactly the maximum time it will take for a message to reach its destination, or even set an upper limit.

Think of systems that require a response in a limited time. It is what is known as real time systems. There are all kinds, from machinery control systems to multimedia systems.

Critical Real Time Systems (Hard Real-Time Systems). A control system of a robot, an airplane, or a helicopter cannot raise the indefinite retransmission of messages. If there is a problem, it must be treated in time to guarantee the safety of the users and the physical integrity of the device at all times. Sometimes the response times cannot exceed a handful of microseconds, and if it does not respond in time, the result can be fatal. These types of systems cannot be treated with GNU / Linux, as we have seen so far. We do not rule out a future book for this type of system, but it certainly goes beyond the objectives of the current course.

Soft Real-Time Systems. In other cases, the answer in a limited time is desirable but has no catastrophic consequences if it is not met. It is the case of multimedia systems. When voice and video communications are made, it is desirable that the arrival rate be more or less constant and, above all, that delays of more than the duration of the buffer do not accumulate. If it is not fulfilled, we will see cuts in the video and annoying metallic clicks in the audio. These types of systems can be treated without problems with GNU / Linux, but TCP is usually not the best possible option.

Unreliable Datagram Protocol

All real-time systems have a common requirement: they need to reduce latency to the minimum possible. Latency is the time that passes from when a message is sent until it is delivered at the other end.

To address these problems, there is a complementary protocol of TCP, the Unreliable Datagram Protocol (UDP). In UDP, there is no flow control; there are no retransmissions; there is no reordering; there is nothing more than routing and guarantee of integrity. I mean, we know how to take the messages to their destination, and if they arrive, they are sure to be sent. That's it. They can arrive in a different order from the delivery, and they can get lost along the way, they can even be duplicated. And the emissary will never have any feedback on whether the message has been received correctly or not. Little, right?

The positive part is that the latency, especially in networks with losses or congested, is significantly lower. So, it is used for video and audio broadcast. Because of its simplicity, it is also often used to communicate with very small devices (8-bit microcontrollers, FPGAs, etc.). All necessary guarantees remain the responsibility of the application. For example, if you need confirmations, you must send UDP messages requesting those confirmations.

Well, enough theory, get to work. Prepare the two terminals as in the case of the previous TCP communication and execute the following in the first.

pi @ raspberrypi: ~ $ nc -u -l 8888

This is the UDP server. Server is the name of the passive role in communication, the one that waits. That doesn't mean he doesn't talk, but he doesn't speak until someone (a client) starts a conversation. On the other terminal run the client:

pi @ raspberrypi: ~ $ nc -u 127.0.0.1 8888

Try to transfer data in both directions. As you can see, it works in a very similar way, and you will not be able to appreciate the difference if you do not use relatively distant equipment and somewhat congested networks. For the purposes of the book, they are practically equivalent, and we will opt for one or the other according to the requirements of the application.

Wireshark

When network communications are used, problems of all kinds appear very frequently. How do we diagnose them? The easiest way is to use a traffic capture and analysis tool. On your Raspberry Pi, you already have one of the best tools available: Wireshark.

Wireshark Initial Screen
When starting, the application shows something similar to the figure. A list appears with the network interfaces that we already know and some more that escapes what is intended with this book. Select the loopback interface: lo and press Start.

Now repeat the example of TCP and UDP communication we have done in this chapter. It is interesting even to make a mistake on purpose. Try, for example, to run the UDP client without a server at the other end.

Message Capture from the * Loopback * Interface

The normal thing in a network is to see hundreds of packages, and it is relatively difficult to find what we want to examine. That's why Wireshark incorporates very advanced filtering features. For the capture by clicking on the red square button, and we will filter the packages that interest us. For example, we will see the TCP packets destined for the port you have used. To do this, click Expression... You will have a dialog like the one in the figure in which you can write TCP to find all the TCP fields.

Capture Filter Editing

Display all the TCP protocol parameters and select tcp.port. In the Relation column, choose ==, and in the Value column, choose the port number you used. To finish press OK. Now, you will see in the Filter box the expression you have selected, some of the style at tcp.port == 3040. But we have not yet applied it. Press the button Apply. Only the conversation that interests us appears. As you can see, things are more complicated than they seem:

TCP conversation with a single message (Len other than 0).

The first three messages are the connection establishment (triple handshake), and until the fourth message, we do not see what we have sent. In the center window, the different elements of each captured message are dissected.

Another very useful option is full flow tracking. Right-click on any of the messages at the top of the screen and select the Follow TCP Stream option in the context menu that appears.

TCP Flow Tracking

The entire data exchange sequence appears without all the TCP paraphernalia. Only the data. In blue in one direction and in red in the other. In addition, we can select only the traffic in one of the directions. This is extraordinarily useful when we want to replicate the behavior of other programs.

Networking

The history of communication networks between computers is closely related to the history of Unix and, therefore, indirectly with GNU / Linux. At the University of California, Berkeley, the original idea of Unix, in which everything is an archive, was generalized to the networks. Communications are scheduled very similar to the use of files. These special files are called sockets.

The socket- based programming interface (API socket) remains the dominant one today to deal with communications networks and is the one we will see in the corresponding chapter.

In any case, it is convenient to give some small notions of the general fundamentals before writing code. In the introduction to GNU, in chapter 1 of this book, we already talk about file descriptors. These are numbers that represent the files from the point of view of the operating system. They basically provide an interface based on four basic operations, which correspond to system calls (operating system services):

The open call opens a file. Search for the file in the file system using a hierarchical name called the file path and assign a new file descriptor. From this moment, we can forget the route. The operating system only needs the descriptor. The close call closes the file. With this, the operating system terminates all ongoing operations that affect the file and releases its descriptor so that it can be reused with another file. The write call writes a set of octets to the file, and the read call reads a set of octets from the file.

This programming interface is used in GNU for a multitude of operations, operations with files on the disk, writing messages on the terminal, reading data from the keyboard, reading mouse events, etc. It seems logical that it also extends to network communications programming, and that is what the socket interface does.

A network connection does not have any element on the disk that represents it. Therefore, there is no choice but to replace the open call with another equivalent that provides the information necessary for communication. That call is called socket and is what gives name to the programming interface.

The so-called socket assigns a file descriptor to a communication channel. But the communication channel is not enough, and we need to provide the data about the recipient or the origin of each message (IP addresses used, TCP or UDP ports, etc.). This is done with a new connect call for the client side or bind for the server side. When the socket is connected, it already works as a normal file descriptor.

From that moment on, all file descriptor calls are also valid (read, write, and close are also operations that can be performed on sockets once they are connected).

UDP communications do not need more calls, that's all. It is so similar that in some operating systems such as Plan9 or 2k, sockets are created with open calls using a special file path. However, GNU provides other sendto or recvfrom calls that only combine the write call with the connect call and the read call with the bind call. We will not use them at all.

However, TCP is more complex. To provide additional guarantees, the concept of connection needs to be implemented, such as the establishment of a new single channel between the two communicating processes. On the client side, it's simple; just connect do this job. The connection, in this case, is not simply to assign the destination address but to reserve a series of resources for communication with the destination.

The TCP server side is the most complex. Each client that connects to the server must have its own connection. With socket and bind, we can create a socket that serves messages destined for a specific address and a specific port, but only one. The solution goes through one more call, accept, which creates another new socket on each connection from a client process. The API is completed with a listen call that must be invoked to configure how many almost simultaneous connections it is possible to handle.

Although there are many more details that we have not mentioned, I think it can be used to understand how communications are programmed. These tables can be used to understand the sequence of operations that must be performed.

Chapter 9 - C Development

For the first time, the book will be held in a multi-language version (C and Python). We hope in this way to accommodate a greater number of students. Currently, we use Python as the first language of the degree (first semester of the first year, Computer Science subject), but until this course, we have used C. Therefore, there is a group of students who feel more comfortable with C and another that feels more comfortable with Python.

This book tries to divide the content so that you don't have to read everything if you are interested in only one of these languages. In this chapter, we will describe the set of tools that we will use to make C programs and a simple example of their use.

The First Program

It is tradition to start with a first program that simply writes the message Hello, World on the screen. It goes back to the origins of BCPL, the precursor of C.

Start an order terminal and create a folder to enter the examples in this chapter. We will work in that folder. For example:

pi @ raspberrypi: ~ $ mkdir test
pi @ raspberrypi: ~ $ cd test
Raspberry Pi pi @: ~ / test $ ▄

Use a text editor to write the following program in a file named hello.c. As a text editor
you can use Leafpad, simply by clicking on the icon or from the command line with Leafpad hello.c.

```
#include <stdio.h>
int main () {
puts ("Hello, World");
return 0;
}
```

Save the file to the folder you created and return to the terminal:

pi @ raspberrypi: ~ / test $ make hello
cc hello.c -o hello Raspberry Pi pi @: ~ / test $ _

The C program has been compiled by GNU make (make), which in turn has run the C (cc) compiler to generate the hello executable. Note that GNU executables do not have a distinctive extension.

Now we can execute it:

pi @ raspberrypi: ~ / test $./hello
Hello World
Raspberry Pi pi @: ~ / test $ _

Notice that we have written a period and a bar in front to indicate where the file is located. It is a relative route, of which we have already spoken.

You will wonder why we have to indicate the path for this executable and not for Leafpad, for example. The operational system finds the executables either because the user explicitly tells them where they are or because they are in a series of folders that are known as system paths. Obviously, the current folder is not in the system paths, because you just created it, so our only option is to indicate the path.
Warning You may read texts that recommend you add the folder. (the work folder) to the system paths. Do not do it, it is a bad idea in general, but especially for security reasons.

The C Compiler

In GNU / Linux, there are several C compilers. The most used is that of the GNU (GNU Compiler Collection) project that is invoked with the gcc or simply cc command. Normally we will not compile the C files by hand, but we will do it through a construction tool, specifically GNU make.

The C compiler can be used as a compiler, as an editor or as both. For example, back to our program hello.c and type in the terminal the following:

pi @ raspberrypi: ~ / test $ gcc -c hello.c
pi @ raspberrypi: ~ / test $ ls
hello hello.c hello.o
Raspberry Pi pi @: ~ / test $ ▄

Now we have a hello.o file. It is an object file with the machine instructions corresponding to the hello.c file but without the structure of an executable. Multiple object files can be combined to generate a single executable using the editor. In GNU you can use the C compiler itself to mount the executable:

pi @ raspberrypi: ~ / test $ gcc -o hello hello.o
Raspberry Pi pi @: ~ / test $ ▄
When we do not use the -c option, the compiler behaves as an editor and, if necessary, as a compiler simultaneously. If we do not specify an executable name with the -o option, the compiler will generate one with a.out name. This is so for historical reasons, so it is clear that we usually must specify the -o option.

Multiple Source Files

An executable can be composed from several source files. For example, divide the program into a hello.c file which has the main program and uses a function that is defined in another

89

file named fc:

```
#include <stdio.h>
void say_hello () {
puts ("Hello, World");
}
```

Now the hello.c file would be something like this:
```
void say_hello (void);
int main () {
say hi();
return 0;
}
```

To generate the executable, you would have to compile both files and then mount them:

```
pi @ raspberrypi: ~ / test $ gcc -c hello.c fc
pi @ raspberrypi: ~ / test $ gcc -o hello hello.o fo
Raspberry Pi pi @: ~ / test $ ▄
```

We are going to change the program so that it greets and says goodbye. In addition to the function say_hello (now in the file f_hola.c) we will have another function say_adios (in the file f_adios.c).

```
pi @ raspberrypi: ~ / test $ mv fc f_hola.c
pi @ raspberrypi: ~ / test $ cp f_hola.c f_adios.c
pi @ raspberrypi: ~ / test $ leafpad f_adios.c
```
Now change the f_adios.c file to say goodbye:
```
#include <stdio.h>
say goodbye () {
puts ("Goodbye, World");
}
```

And the main program hello.c to call the two functions:

```
void say_hello (void);
void say_bye (void);
int main () {
say hi();
say goodbye();
return 0;
}
```

This is more like a real show. The main program calls several functions that are spread over other files. But it is not usual to put the declaration of functions directly in the main file. It is better to put those statements in a header file that is included when needed.

For example, edit a new file greet.h   with the declarations of the two functions:

```
#ifndef SALUDAR_H
#define SALUDAR_H
void say_hello (void);
void say_bye (void);
#endif
And use it in hello.c:
#include "greet.h"
int main () {
say hi();
say goodbye();
return 0;
}
```

Now we can compile everything:

Raspberry Pi pi @: ~ / test $ gcc -c hello.c f_hola.c f_adios.c
Raspberry Pi pi @: ~ / test $ gcc -o hello f_hola.o hello.o f_adios.o

Raspberry Pi pi @: ~ / test $ ▪

Note that the header file does not need to be compiled because it has nothing but declarations and is included where necessary.

Program Libraries

When programs grow, a more flexible organization mechanism becomes necessary. For example, we can group several of the object files in a library and then mount the executable with the library. For example, we are going to put the files f_hola.o and f_adios.o in a libsaludar.a library, and then we build the executable with this library. To create the library, we will use the program ar (archiver):

pi @ raspberrypi: ~ / test $ ar rcs libsaludar.a f_hola.o f_adios.o pi @ raspberrypi: ~ / test $ gcc -L. -o hello hello.o -lsaludar Raspberry Pi pi @: ~ / test $ ▪

The ar program is somewhat similar to the archives that are used to create compressed files (WinZip, WinRAR, 7zip, PeaZip, etc.) unless, in this case, it is not compressed. In GNU, compression and archiving are separate processes, so that the user can choose how to archive and how to compress independently.

In the same libsaludar.a file, we can put any number of object files with any number of functions. However, when building the executable with gcc, things do not change even if the number of files and functions grows.

Libraries are usually made in a separate folder. For example:

pi @ raspberrypi: ~ / test $ mkdir greeting
pi @ raspberrypi: ~ / test $ mv *.h f_ * greeting

pi @ raspberrypi: ~ / test $ cd greeting
pi @ raspberrypi: ~ / test / greeting $ gcc -c *.c
pi @ raspberrypi: ~ / test / greeting $ ar rcs libsaludar.a *.o
pi @ raspberrypi: ~ / test / greeting $ cd..
Raspberry Pi pi @: ~ / test $ ▄

Now the library is in the greeting subfolder and the main program in the parent folder. To compile hello.c we have to tell the compiler where the header files can be and when mounting hello, we must indicate the new folder where to look for libraries:

Raspberry Pi pi @: ~ / test $ gcc -c hello.c -Isaludo
Raspberry Pi pi @: ~ / test $ gcc -o hello -Lsaludo hello.o -lsaludar
Raspberry Pi pi @: ~ / test $

The GNU Make Construction Tool

As we have seen, as soon as the program starts to grow a little, the process of building the executable can be really tedious. The make program that we already used in the first example allows us to automate the construction.

$ (CC) $ (CFLAGS) -c $ <

Anatomy of a Make Recipe.

C Development

Except in the trivial cases, you need a configuration file that tells you how to build the executable. It must be called makefile, Makefile, or GNUmakefile. It basically consists of recipes in which you explain how to build a file from a specified set of files. So, in our last example we can make a makefile inside the greeting subfolder like this one:

```
libsaludar.a: f_hola.o f_adios.o
ar rcs $ @ $ ^
```

This rule reads like this: to build libsaludar.a, you must first build f_hola.o and f_adios.o and then execute ar rcs libsaludar.o f_hola.o f_adios.o. Notice that we use the abbreviation $ @ to represent the purpose of the rule (libsaludar.a) and $ ^ to represent the dependencies of the rule (everything that follows the colon). And how do we tell you how to make the object files f_hola.o and f_adios.o ? It is not necessary. GNU make knows how to make them from C files with the same name. Internally you have already defined a recipe like this:

```
%.o:%.c
$ (CC) $ (CFLAGS) -c $ <
```

That reads to build an object file from a C file of the same name you must execute where the symbol $ < corresponds to a special GNU make variable.

The recipes already included in GNU make it virtually unnecessary to define new rules except in very simple cases. The interesting thing about this is that the make rules use a wide variety of variables that already have a default value, but that we can change to adjust the operation.

Now just run make clean to delete the generated files and leave only the code we have written.

An interesting aspect of the use of make is that it only generates what is necessary, and the rules affected by files that have changed apply. That is, if a good makefile is available, just run make so that everything you need is compiled and only what is necessary at any time.

If the makefile does not have all the dependencies, GNU make will not know if it has to rebuild any file. For example, in this

94

small example, we have not added hello.o dependencies with greeting / greeting.h. The correct thing would have been to add a rule in which only the dependency is indicated:

hello.o: hello.c greeting / greeting.h

If you do not want to complicate makefile just keep it in mind, and when you modify something that is not in the dependencies, we can force the compilation with:

pi @ raspberrypi: ~ / test $ make -C greeting -B
pi @ raspberrypi: ~ / test $ make -B

The first order forces the construction of the library, and the second forces the construction of the executable.

Debugging Programs with GNU Debugger

The construction of correct programs requires the close cooperation of two very simple but very important techniques: testing and debugging.

The test consists in the elaboration of small programs that show that our functions do what they are supposed to do. There is nothing to replace this, and it is essential in any software development process. We will discuss this topic later.

The other technique that complements the test is debugging, which consists in the elimination of errors (bugs) previously detected in the tests. Debugging is a relatively simple process in the form and totally systematic, but surprisingly difficult in practice.

No special tool is needed to debug. A set of carefully chosen printf statements or any other way to examine the contents of the memory can be used. GNU debugger (abbreviated gdb) is therefore not strictly necessary, but it can save you a huge amount of time.

Debugging tools allow you to stop the execution of the program at specific points, for example, just before the occurrence of an error in which it is known that the execution ends unexpectedly. Stopping the program allows you to explore the memory at that point, including knowing the value of the processor's variables and records and moving forward through the execution until you find the exact point at which the program dysfunction occurs.

The Debugging Process

Let's talk a little first about the process of eliminating errors. It is important because experience tells us that it is counter-intuitive, and we naturally tend to skip essential steps.

Program errors can be classified in several ways. It is very common to classify them according to their visibility and persistence:

	Visible	Hidden
Persistent	Ideal	Unknown
Transient	Hard	Very difficult

A visible error is one that has been detected because the program does not do what it should. On the contrary, a hidden error is one that has not been detected, although it exists, either because the code it affects is executed very rarely or because there is another error that masks it. Visible errors are usually detected in tests and do not usually reach the code in production. However, the hidden ones reach the production code and can have disastrous consequences. Ariane 5 or Therac 25 are some examples that we should all remember. Search Google if you don't know them.

On the other hand, they can also be classified as persistent errors when errors manifest themselves in all programs or transient executions when they only manifest in some executions or at unpredictable moments.

Obviously, the ideals for their elimination are visible and persistent errors, and we have to do everything possible so that the possible errors are of this type. For that, defensive programming techniques and memory debugging tools such as Valgrind are used. It is outside the scope of this course to talk about the latter, but we recommend that you try them if you encounter an elusive error.

Usually, the errors are detected in the tests, and even if this is not the case, we should make a small test program that reproduces the error. Therefore, we can assume that there is a relatively short program that does not do what we expect. The key is to apply debugging consistent with the following process:

- Study the data. See which tests fail and which ones succeed.
- Develop a hypothesis consistent with the data.
- Design an experiment to refute the hypothesis. Decide how to interpret the result of the experiment a priori, before performing it.
- Keep a record of everything.

The design stage of the experiment is also very systematic. The aim is to narrow the search space, either by reducing the range of data to be analyzed or by limiting the region of the program where the error is located.

Typically, a small program is designed that exercises the functions that may contain the error. From this failed test case, a binary search of the error is performed. If the program does not work correctly, it is because some of the values returned or stored are not what we expected. Approximately at the midpoint, we will have to check if the intermediate values calculated so far are as expected. If they are correct, the error must be in the second half; otherwise, it would be in the first half. We repeat this process until we find the point of error.

It is at this stage of the debugging process that debuggers such as GNU debugger can be useful. Of course, we can always examine the intermediate values with a printf in the right place. But every time, we have to examine another point we will have to recompile the program. The debugger, on the other hand, allows you to examine and modify any program data and stop the execution of the program at any point.

Using GNU Debugger

In order for gdb to be fully exploited, it is necessary to compile the program with support for debugging. This is specified with the compiler -ggdb option. Typically, it is done by adding this option to the CFLAGS variable of the makefile.

Using the command-line interface, the first step is to invoke gdb specifying the executable to debug:

pi @ raspberrypi: ~ / test $ gdb hello
GNU gdb (Raspbian 7.7.1 + dfsg-5) 7.7.1
...
Reading symbols from hello... done.
(gdb) ▪

Displays the GDB prompt indicating that you wait for an order.

Watchpoints

A watchpoint is an indication to the debugger to interrupt the execution of the program each time the value of a variable is read or modified. Several GDB orders allow us to work with them.

Alter Variables and Flow

It is common for more than one error to be detected in a GDB session. Sometimes it may be interesting to temporarily fix a problem to find another without recompiling. With GDB, it is possible to set values to variables or alter the normal sequence of execution.

Work with Processes

Some of our programs will be multithreaded. GDB allows working with multiple processes simultaneously, even if they correspond to different executables.

Work with Threads

We will also sometimes use the threads. It is a much more efficient concurrency mechanism than processes, but significantly more prone to hard-to-find errors.

Chapter 10 - Programming the Peripherals

We will now see a series of C programming examples of the elements we have seen in Chapter 2. Our goal is to provide an overview of the full range of possibilities we have available using C language. That implies that we are not going to limit to using a library, but all that I know at the moment.

When you face a new project, you have to understand all the elements involved. This usually involves exploring, testing, and reading. Your first objective has to be to reduce uncertainty, to have enough details to avoid having to look at the datasheet of the devices at every step when we are designing the application.

Do not take these examples as a sample of how to program, and we will see that later. It's about learning to use peripherals from your favorite programming language. Therefore, we try to make the code as simple and straightforward as possible, not the most maintainable, not even the most readable. We give priority to the use of the API offered by each library.

Digital Inputs and Outputs in C

For the programming of digital inputs and outputs in C, we have three libraries available: wiringPi by Gordon Henderson, bcm2835 by Mike McCauley, and pigpio by joan@abyz.co.uk. All of them are more or less equivalent for the purposes of the book, although each has its advantages and disadvantages. To start, I recommend you use WiringPi. Let's look at examples with all three.

Digital Inputs and Outputs with WiringPi

Check out the WiringPi reference book and especially the main functions. If you try to execute it, you will probably get a message that indicates that user pi does not have enough privileges. In that case, you have to run it with sudo. This is going to be quite frequent in software that manipulates physical devices.

No serious operating system can allow a normal user to directly manipulate the devices. It could even compromise the physical integrity of the system.

We can also program the generation of PWM signals with the help of the WiringPi library. The base frequency for PWM in Raspberry Pi is 19.2Mhz. This frequency can be divided by using a divisor indicated with pwmSetClock, up to a maximum of 4095. At this frequency the internal algorithm that generates the sequence of pulses, but in the case of the BCM2835 are two operating modes, a mode balanced (balanced) which is difficult to control the pulse width, but allows a PWM control very high frequency, and a mode mark and space which is much more intuitive and more appropriate to control servos. The balanced mode is appropriate for controlling the power supplied to the load or for transmitting information.

In the mark and space mode, the PWM module will increase an internal counter until it reaches a configurable limit, the PWM range, which can be a maximum of 1024. At the beginning of the cycle, the pin will be set to 1 logical and will remain until the internal counter reaches the value set by the user. At that time, the pin will be set to 0 logical and will remain until the end of the cycle.

Let's see its application to the control of a servomotor. A servomotor has a signal input to indicate the desired inclination. Every 20ms expect a pulse, and the width of this pulse determines the inclination of the servo. Around 1.5ms is the pulse width necessary for the centered position. A smaller width rotates the servo counterclockwise (up to approximately 1ms), and a longer duration makes it rotate clockwise (up to approximately 2ms). In this case, the range and the divisor must be calculated so that the pulse is produced every 20ms, and the control of the pulse width around 1.5ms is with the maximum possible resolution.

The assembly is as following. The red servo cable (V +) is connected to + 5V in P1-2 or P1-4, the black or brown cable (V-) to GND in P1-6, and the yellow, orange, or white (signal) cable to GPIO18 on P1-12. No other components are needed.

```
#include <wiringPi.h>
#include <stdlib.h>
int main (int argc, char * argv [])
{
if (argc <5) {
printf ("Usage:% s divisor range min max \ n", argv [0]);
exit (0);
}
int div = atoi (argv [1]);
int range = atoi (argv [2]);
int min = atoi (argv [3]);
int max = atoi (argv [4]);
wiringPiSetupGpio ();
pinMode (18, PWM_OUTPUT);
pwmSetMode (PWM_MODE_MS);
pwmSetClock (div);
pwmSetRange (range);
for (;;) {
pwmWrite (18, min);
delay (1000);
pwmWrite (18, max);
delay (1000);
}
}
```

To have maximum control of the servo position, we will test with the maximum range of 1024. In that case, the divisor must be such that the frequency of the PWM pulse is:

$$f = \frac{\text{base } f}{\text{range} \times \text{div}} = \frac{19.2 \times 10^6 \, \text{Hz}}{1024 \times \text{div}} = \frac{1}{20 \, \text{ms}} = 50 \, \text{Hz}$$

That is, the splitter should be set to 390. The full range of the servo depends on the specific model. Theoretically, it should be between 52 and 102, the value being fully centered 77. In practice, the specific servo will have to be tested. Our experiments give a useful range between 29 and 123 for the TowerPro microservo available in the laboratory.

Programming Digital Inputs and Outputs with BCM2835

The bcm2835 library is a very fine wrapper of hardware capabilities. That is, it practically describes in C what appears on the Broadcom datasheet. In this sense, it is ideal to explore the architecture and extract the maximum juice from your Raspberry Pi. For non-trivial tasks, you will have no choice but to study well to understand how it works.

As for the handling of digital inputs and outputs, the bcm2835 library has an interface very similar to WiringPi but supports many more capabilities of the underlying hardware. In this book, we will not use the advanced features.

An interesting feature of the programs that use bcm2835 is that they do not need to be executed as superuser if they only access the GPIO pins, it is enough that the user belongs to the gpio group.

```
#include <bcm2835.h>
int main () {
bcm2835_init ();
bcm2835_gpio_fsel (18, BCM2835_GPIO_FSEL_OUTP);
for (int v = 0;; v =! v) {
bcm2835_gpio_write (18, v);
bcm2835_delay (1000);
}
bcm2835_close ();
}
```

As you can see, the code is practically equivalent to wiringPi. The compilation is also similar. To compile it, we can make a makefile file almost equivalent to the wiringPi example.

```
CFLAGS = -I / usr / local / include
LDFLAGS = -L / usr / local / lib
LDLIBS = -lbcm2835
test-gpio: test-gpio.o
```

Regardless of the name of the library, we see that it is necessary to indicate that you look for header files in / usr / local / include and look for the libraries in / usr / local / lib. This is because bcm2835 is not yet as a system package, and we have installed it manually.

Among the advanced features bcm2835 implements the possibility of changing the value of a set of hit pins, of reading a set of hit pins, better control over the events of rising, falling, or leveling flank events, etc.

PWM with BCM2835

When programming, the pulse width modulation bcm2835 requires a little knowledge of the hardware operation. For example, it requires knowing that the two PWM channels are not associated with a single pin and that one or the other channel can be associated with some of the pins by selecting specific alternative functions. Following the same example of wiringPi, we will configure the GPIO18 pin as PWM output. For this, we will have to select the alternative function 5 of that pin, which corresponds to the PWM0 channel. Do you understand now the utility of the flyer that we give you in the book? From that moment, we only work with the channel, not with the pin.

```c
#include <bcm2835.h>
#include <stdio.h>
int main (int argc, char * argv [])
{
if (argc <5) {
printf ("Usage:% s divisor range min max \ n", argv [0]);
exit (0);
}
int div = atoi (argv [1]);
int range = atoi (argv [2]);
int min = atoi (argv [3]);
int max = atoi (argv [4]);
bcm2835_init ();
bcm2835_gpio_fsel (18, BCM2835_GPIO_FSEL_ALT5);
bcm2835_pwm_set_clock (div);
bcm2835_pwm_set_mode (0, 1, 1);
bcm2835_pwm_set_range (0, range);
for (;;) {
bcm2835_pwm_set_data (0, min);
bcm2835_delay (1000);
bcm2835_pwm_set_data (0, max);
bcm2835_delay (1000);
}
bcm2835_close ();
return 0;
}
```

Programming Digital Inputs and Outputs with Pigpio

The pigpio library is halfway between the previous two. On the one hand, it implements a low-level interface that practically reproduces the Broadcom data-sheet in C. On the other hand. It implements abstraction layers that extend the functionality considerably. For example, it adds the possibility to simulate PWM modulation on any pin and incorporates very interesting debugging capabilities.

From the point of view of programming digital inputs and outputs, it is very similar to the other libraries.

```
#include <pigpio.h>
int main () {
gpioInitialise ();
gpioSetMode (18, PI_OUTPUT);
for (int v = 0;; v =! v) {
gpioWrite (18, v);
gpioDelay (1000000);
}
gpioTerminate ();
}
```

Virtually identical to the other examples except for the names of the functions. The compilation is very similar to the examples in bcm2835 because the pigpio library is also not available as a system package, and we have had to install it manually.

```
CFLAGS = -I / usr / local / include -pthread
LDFLAGS = -L / usr / local / lib -pthread
LDLIBS = -lpigpio -lpthread
test-gpio: test-gpio.o
```

An important difference with respect to the other libraries is that you have to enable the use of threads and add the system's thread library. This is necessary because many of the added capabilities of pigpio are implemented as threads.

PWM Modulation with Pigpio

PWM modulation with pigpio can be done with low-level functions equivalent to what is done in bcm2835 but also supports a much simpler high-level interface. There is a function to control servos with PWM and another to control the duty-cycle, and with it, the power delivered to a load.

It is not necessary to specify low-level parameters, just the pulse width in milliseconds. A width of zero for the PWM signal. The remaining valid values are between 500 and 2500, although the actual servo range depends on the specific model.

Another interesting feature of pigpio is that these functions can be applied to any pin. If it is one of those that supports PWM by hardware, it will use it transparently and, if not, simulate it with a separate thread. The frequency of the PWM signal it generates is, in all cases, 50Hz.

Exercises

Do not try to use all libraries at once. Choose one and wait to feel comfortable with it to try another. At the moment, we propose the following exercises.
1.   Configure and program the hardware and software necessary to have two LEDs flashing at the same rate but keeping only one of them on at the same time.
2.   Modify the previous example so that switching takes place only when a button is pressed. One of the LEDs will be on when the button is not pressed, and the other will be on only when the button is pressed.

Challenges for the Week

1.   Moderate: Design a mechanism to control an array of LEDs of at least 16x32 with the Raspberry Pi.

Chapter 11 - I2C Interface Programming

The precise programming of an I2C device depends a lot on the manufacturer. In general, we will first need a configuration, and then we will enter a loop that reads or writes data. For example, let's see how the MPU6050 accelerometer is handled.
I2C programming with wiringPi
As always, wiringPi sacrifices flexibility for the sake of greater simplicity. It does not even provide a function to change the clock frequency and does not support block transfers, but only 8 and 16-bit registers.

I2C Programming with BCM2835

In bcm2835, the interface is also simple, but a file descriptor is not required for each I2C device, and the communication is a bit cumbersome because the addressing of the records must be done manually with a write.

Actually, the library supports some other functions to deal with special cases. If you face a new I2C module, consult the documentation of bcm2835 in case it makes things easier for you.

I2C Programming with Pigpio

The pigpio library implements an interface that combines the two previous approaches. You can read or write bytes or words, but also blocks, which significantly simplifies the program. It also allows access to the two I2C buses.

As in the rest of the pigpio modules, it is the most complete of the three, and bcm2835 is the closest to the hardware and, therefore, the smallest. Our personal recommendation is that you use wiringPi to start, for its simplicity.

Chapter 12 – SPI C Programming

The three libraries we have used for programming digital inputs and outputs also support the use of the SPI interface. SPI modules benefit from concurrent sending and receiving capacity, and very reasonable rates (30MHz) can be achieved

SPI Programming with WiringPi

Programming is simple in that it only uses two functions, but it can be really complicated to understand communication with some SPI devices. The reason is that in SPI to be able to read data, and you have to write data; in fact, it is read at the same time it is written. This means that in real devices, you have to make many transactions that are completely discarded.

The wiringPiSPISetup function initializes the communication for channel 0 to 10Mz. There are two channels available (0 and 1) that use the same legs except for the selection SPI_CE0 and SPI_CE1, respectively.
Calls to wiringPiSPIDataRW to perform an SPI transaction where a concurrent set of bytes is written and read. The precise meaning of what is read and written depends on the device and in some cases may require discarding part or all of the information. In this case, the first byte is the order, and then the arguments are sent.
Simplicity is maximum, but hardware capabilities are also lost to accommodate all SPI transfer modes. More details can be found in the Gordon Henderson article available at projects.drogon.net.

The problem with wiringPi is that for SPI transfers, it is not possible to select the mode. The author considers that the vast majority of SPI modules use mode 0. It may be true, but the ADS1118 we use in the book is mode 1.

Warning The wiringPi library assumes that we use SPI0 with mode 0. For this reason, we do not recommend it because the CJMCU-1118 module uses mode 1.

SPI Programming with BCM2835

In the bcm2835 library, we have a range of functions closer to hardware. Some functions are similar to wiringPi, but it adds many more to configure the transfer mode and the SPI interface.

Although it seems more complex, it is really due to the greater control of initialization. Initialization is longer, but the possibility of using different transmission and reception buffers simplifies many frequent cases.

SPI Programming with Pigpio

With pigpio, it is possible to use the auxiliary peripheral SPI (SPI1) in addition to the main one (see flag A of the flag field in spiOpen). The advantage is that this other SPI interface has configurable word size and three available chip lines (instead of two). On the other hand, the main interface is noticeably faster, so we will use that normally.

Measure Times Accurately

The measurement of the discharge time of a capacitor has been proposed as a technique to measure analog quantities using the digital inputs of the Raspberry Pi. Adafruit's proposal uses the number of iterations of a loop to measure time. As they themselves recognize, this is not very accurate.

Raspbian is a timeshare system. The Raspberry Pi runs several programs at once, and this implies that the processor can evict our program to run another program. In that case, the number of iterations of the loop will be significantly less than normal. But how do we know if there has been eviction? The sad reality is that a user program cannot know it; it has no control over this. This is not even the only cause of uncertainty, and there may be interference from interrupt handlers, device handlers, etc.

But there is a way to measure time quite accurately, using the MISO leg of the SPI interface and a digital output leg.

Suppose we have a sensor device whose measurement materializes in the value of a resistor. It can be an LDR, as in the case of the Adafruit article, or a simple potentiometer, or a thermistor, or a piezoresistive sensor, or a magnetoresistive sensor,... We build an RC circuit similar to the figure.

We discharge the condenser by putting the GPIO22 leg low for a sufficient time. We configure the GPIO22 leg as an input so that it is high impedance, and we start a large SPI transfer. The buffer must be full of zeros until the capacitor charge is sufficient to be interpreted as a 1. The first non-zero byte marks the instant in which the capacitor is reasonably charged. This time is proportional to RC, and, therefore, to R. A calibration can be performed to measure with absolute precision, but in any case, we have a precise measurement that allows us to compare.

The code is extremely simple. We provide it only in wiringPi.

Assembly for precise measurement of a resistor.
The program prints the buffer position where the input begins to be nonzero and the first nonzero value. That position would have to be multiplied by 8 to translate it into SCLK cycles and could be adjusted with the value to obtain the exact number of cycles.

The accuracy depends on the clock period used. In the example, we have used a 500KHz clock, but it can be up to 32MHz safely. The problem is that the larger the clock, the greater the buffer we have to use in the SPI transfer.

For buffers larger than 4KB, you must specify it in the kernel command line (/boot/cmdline.txt) and restart the Raspberry Pi. For example, for 256KB, it would be added:

spidev.bufsiz = 262144

The code can be improved by a bisection search. It is deliberately simple to be understood from the conceptual point of view. The result is that we could measure RC with an accuracy of up to 1/32 us. If we use a 1uF capacitor, this implies that we can measure R with an accuracy of 1/32 Ohm. Even if we use the 500KHz clock, we will have an accuracy of 2 Ohm, which is also not bad.

Actual results may be somewhat worse due to jitter or instability in SCLK or resistance noise. A ceramic capacitor in parallel with the electrolytic can help remove high frequency noise. In any case, the method is much more precise than Adafruit's original proposal, and does not depend on the state of loading of the system.

Challenges for the Week

1. Easy Design a mechanism to control LED strips using the SPI interface.

Chapter 13 - udp_server_socket: Network Communications

Both B +, 2B, and 3B models include an Ethernet interface. The Raspberry Pi 4 B that we use in this book includes WiFi, but any of the others can also have WiFi for a price of about € 4 using a USB WiFi interface. Therefore, any Raspberry Pi project must consider the possibility of communicating data through a TCP / IP network.

To program on a network in GNU / Linux, as in most modern operating systems, a programming interface called API socket is used. It is a set of functions designed to make network programming closely resemble input / output with files.

In chapter 2, we have already introduced the socket interface. In C, this interface is included in the libc system library that is automatically incorporated.

Conclusion

Thank you for making it through to the end of *Raspberry Pi 4 Ultimate Guide*, let's hope it was informative and able to provide you with all of the tools you need to achieve your goals whatever they may be.

The Raspberry Pi, a small single board computer, also called a nano-computer, has gathered a considerable community around it. The many features available have delighted the makers and electronics enthusiasts of all kinds. Each new version of this software is always eagerly awaited.

Released recently, the new Raspberry Pi 4 convinces with its ARM Cortex-A72 1.5 GHz. In this new model, it is also possible to add 1 GB, 2 GB or even 4 GB of RAM, greatly increasing its computing power.

Some important interface changes make the Raspberry Pi a must-have. In particular, it has a LAN Gigabit LAN with up to 1000 Mbit and Bluetooth 5.0. Highly anticipated innovations in USB interfaces have emerged: in addition to the usual two USB 2.0 ports, the Raspberry Pi contains two USB 3.0 ports, as well as two micro HDMI interfaces compatible with 4K.

This book was an attempt to guide you to understand Raspberry Pi 4 a lot better and enjoy programming with it.

Finally, if you found this book useful in any way, a review on Amazon is always appreciated!

Description

This practical guide of the Raspberry-Pi 4 is a document that aims to help you get to know and master your Raspberry-Pi 4 a lot better. To do this, the guide steers you step by step to begin and then implement as easily as possible many practical and inexpensive achievements!

You can set up:
- A media center,
- A HiFi system,
- A download server,
- A personal cloud solution,
- An "Old School" console emulator,
- Using the GPIO (New) pins,
- A network supervisor,
- And a lot more...

You will also find all the necessary command lines and tips and tricks to master your small machine.

So, add this book to your cart today and enter the amazing world of Raspberry-Pi 4!!!

www.ingramcontent.com/pod-product-compliance
Lightning Source LLC
Chambersburg PA
CBHW060932220326
41597CB00020BA/3723